SAMUEL L. BRE

HELPS TO HOLINESS

Bob Hostetler, General Editor

wesleyan
PUBLISHING HOUSE
wphstore.com

CREST BOOKS

Copyright © 2016 by The Salvation Army
Published by Wesleyan Publishing House
Indianapolis, Indiana 46250
Printed in the United States of America
ISBN: 978-1-63257-064-2
ISBN (e-book): 978-1-63257-065-9

Library of Congress Cataloging-in-Publication Data

Brengle, Samuel Logan, 1860-1936.
Helps to holiness / Samuel L. Brengle ; Bob Hostetler, general editor.
    pages cm. -- (Samuel L. Brengle's holy life series)
Originally published: London : Simpkin, Marshall, Hamilton, Kent & co., ltd.,
1896.
ISBN 978-1-63257-064-2 (pbk.)
1. Holiness. I. Hostetler, Bob, 1958- editor. II. Title.
BT767.B8 2016
234'.8--dc23

                                                    2015025625

Contents

Preface

Samuel Logan Brengle was an influential author, teacher, and preacher on the doctrine of holiness in the late nineteenth to early twentieth century, serving from 1887–1931 as an active officer (minister) in The Salvation Army. In 1889 while he and his wife, Elizabeth Swift Brengle, were serving as corps officers (pastors) in Boston, Massachusetts, a brick thrown by a street "tough" smashed Brengle's head against a door frame and caused an injury severe enough to require more than nineteen months of convalescence. During that treatment and recuperation period, he began writing articles on holiness for The Salvation Army's publication, *The War Cry*, which were later collected and published as a "little red book" under the title *Helps to Holiness*. That book's success led to eight others over the next forty-five years: *Heart Talks on Holiness*, *The Way of Holiness*, *The Soul-Winner's Secret*, *When the Holy Ghost Is Come*, *Love-Slaves*, *Resurrection Life and Power*,

Ancient Prophets and Modern Problems, and *The Guest of the Soul* (published in his retirement in 1934).

By the time of his death in 1936, Commissioner Brengle was an internationally renowned preacher and worldwide ambassador of holiness. His influence continues today, perhaps more than any Salvationist in history besides the founders, William and Catherine Booth. I hope that the revised and updated editions of his books that comprise the Samuel L. Brengle's Holy Life Series will enhance and enlarge that influence, introduce these writings to new readers, and create fresh interest in those who already know the godly wisdom and life-changing power of these volumes.

While I have taken care to preserve the integrity, impact, and voice of the original writing, I have carefully and prayerfully made changes that I hope will facilitate greater understanding and appreciation of Brengle's words for modern readers. These changes include:

- Revising archaic terms (such as the use of King James English) and updating the language to reflect more contemporary usage (such as occasionally employing more inclusive gender references);
- Shortening and simplifying sentence structure and revising punctuation to conform more closely to contemporary practice;
- Explaining specific references of The Salvation Army that will not be familiar to the general population;
- Updating Scripture references (when possible retaining the King James Version—used exclusively in Brengle's writings—but frequently incorporating modern versions, especially when doing so will aid the reader's comprehension and enjoyment);

- Replacing Roman numerals with Arabic numerals and spelled out Scripture references for the sake of those who are less familiar with the Bible;
- Citing Scripture quotes not referenced in the original and noting the sources for quotes, lines from hymns, etc.;
- Aligning all quoted material to the source (Brengle, who often quoted not only Scripture, but also poetry from memory, often quoted loosely in speaking and writing);
- Adding occasional explanatory phrases or endnotes to identify people or events that might not be familiar to modern readers;
- Revising or replacing some chapter titles, and (in *Ancient Prophets and Modern Problems*) moving one chapter to later in the book; and
- Deleting the prefaces that introduced each book and epigraphs that preceded some chapters.

In the preface to Brengle's first book, Commissioner (later General) Bramwell Booth wrote, "This book is intended to help every reader of its pages into the immediate enjoyment of Bible holiness. Its writer is an officer of The Salvation Army who, having a gracious experience of the things whereof he writes, has been signally used of God, both in life and testimony, to the sanctifying of the Lord's people, as well as in the salvation of sinners. I commend him and what he has here written down to every lover of God and His kingdom here on earth."

In the preface to Brengle's last book, *The Guest of the Soul*, The Salvation Army's third general (and successor to Bramwell Booth) wrote: "These choice contributions . . . will, I am sure, serve to strengthen the faith of the readers of this book and impress upon them the joyousness of life when the heart has been opened to the Holy Guest of the Soul."

I hope and pray that this updated version of Brengle's writings will further those aims.

—Bob Hostetler

general editor

Introduction

On January 9, 1885, at about nine o'clock in the morning, God sanctified my soul. I was in my own room at the time, but in a few minutes I went out and met a man and told him what God had done for me. The next morning, I met another friend on the street and told him the story. He shouted and praised God and urged me to preach full salvation and confess it everywhere. God used him to encourage and help me. So the following day I preached on the subject as clearly and forcibly as I could, and ended with my testimony.

God mightily blessed the Word to others, but I think He blessed it most to me. That confession put me on record. It cut down the bridges behind me. Three worlds were now looking at me as one who professed that God had given him a clean heart. I could not go back now. I had to go forward. God saw that I meant to be true till death. So two mornings after that, just as I got out of bed and was reading some of Jesus' words,

He gave me such a blessing as I never had dreamed a man could have this side of heaven: a heaven of love came into my heart. I walked out over Boston Common before breakfast weeping for joy and praising God. Oh, how I loved! In that hour I knew Jesus, and I loved Him till it seemed my heart would break with love. I loved the sparrows; I loved the dogs; I loved the horses; I loved the little urchins on the streets; I loved the strangers who hurried past me; I loved the whole world.

Do you want to know what holiness is? It is pure love. Do you want to know what the baptism of the Holy Spirit is? It is not a mere sentiment. It is not a happy sensation that passes away in a night. It is a baptism of love that brings every thought into captivity to the Lord Jesus (see 2 Cor. 10:5); casts out all fear (see 1 John 4:18); burns up doubt and unbelief as fire burns flax; makes you "meek and lowly in heart" (Matt. 11:29 KJV); makes you hate uncleanness, lying and deceit, a flattering tongue, and every evil way with a perfect hatred; makes heaven and hell eternal realities; makes you patient and gentle with the disobedient and sinful; makes you "pure . . . peaceable . . . open to reason, full of mercy and good fruits, impartial and sincere" (James 3:17 ESV), and brings you into perfect and unbroken sympathy with the Lord Jesus Christ in His toil and travail to bring a lost and rebellious world back to God.

Oh, how I had longed to be pure! Oh, how I had hungered and thirsted for God—the living God! And He did all that for me. He gave me the desire of my heart. He satisfied me—I weigh my words—He satisfied me!

All the years since then have been wonderful. God has become my teacher, my guide, my counselor, and my all in all.

He has allowed me to be perplexed and tempted, but it has been for my good. I have no complaint to make against Him. Sometimes it has seemed that He left me alone, but it has been as the mother who stands away from her little child to teach him to use his own legs that he may walk. He has not suffered me to fall.

He has helped me to speak of Jesus and His great salvation in such a way so as to instruct, comfort, and save other souls. He has been light to my darkness, strength to my weakness, wisdom in my foolishness, and knowledge in my ignorance.

When my way has been hedged up and it seemed that no way could be found out of my temptations and difficulties, He has cut a way through for me, just as He opened the Red Sea for Israel.

When my heart has ached, He has comforted me. When my feet have nearly slipped, He has held me up. When my faith has trembled, He has encouraged me. When I have been in desperate need, He has supplied every necessity. When I have been hungry, He has fed me. When I have thirsted, He has given me living water.

What has He not done for me? What has He not been to me? I recommend Him to the world. He has taught me that sin is the only thing that can harm me, and that the only thing that can profit me is "faith working through love" (Gal. 5:6 ESV). He has taught me to hang upon Jesus by faith for my salvation from all sin and fear and shame, and to show my love by obeying Him in all things and by seeking in all ways to lead others to obey Him.

I praise Him! I adore Him! I love Him! My whole being is His for time and eternity. I am not my own. He can do with me as He pleases, for I am His. I know that what He chooses must work out for my eternal good.

He is too wise to make mistakes and too good to do me evil. I trust Him, I trust Him, I trust Him! "My hope is from him" (Ps. 62:5 ESV), not from others, not from myself, but from Him. I know He will never fail me.

Since that long-past January day, God has enabled me to keep a perfect, unbroken purpose to serve Him with my whole heart. No temptation has caused me to swerve from that steadfast purpose. No worldly or ecclesiastical ambition has had an atom of weight to allure me. My whole heart has cried within me, as Ephraim's did, "What have I to do any more with idols? I have heard him, and observed him" (Hos. 14:8 KJV).

"Holiness to the LORD" (Ex. 28:36 KJV) has been my motto. In fact, it has been the only motto that could express the deep desire and aspiration of my soul.

For a year and a half at a stretch, I have been laid aside from work by physical weakness. At one time, I would have thought this to be a cross too heavy to bear. But in this, as in all things, God's grace was sufficient.

Lately, God has been blessing me even more. My heart pants after Him and, as I seek Him in fervent, patient, believing prayer and in diligent searching of His Word, He is deepening the work of grace in my soul.

—Samuel L. Brengle

Holiness—What Is It? 1

God's Word commands His people: "Be holy!" (1 Pet. 1:16 NIV).
It says, "It is God's will that you should be sanctified. . . . For God did
not call us to be impure, but to live a holy life" (1 Thess. 4:3, 7 NIV).
It goes so far as to say, "Without holiness no one will see the Lord"
(Heb. 12:14 NIV).

Anyone who reads the Bible in sincerity, not "handling the word
of God deceitfully" (2 Cor. 4:2 KJV), will see that it plainly teaches that
God expects His people to be holy, and that we must be holy to be
happy and useful here and to enter the kingdom of heaven hereafter.
Once a Christian is convinced that the Bible teaches these facts and that
this is God's will, he or she will next inquire, "What is this holiness?
When can I get it, and how?"

There is much difference of opinion on all these points, although the
Bible is simple and plain on each one to every honest seeker of truth.

The Bible tells us that holiness is perfect deliverance from sin. "The blood of Jesus . . . cleanses us from *all* sin" (1 John 1:7 NLT, emphasis added). Not one bit of sin is left, for your old self is crucified with Him, "that the body of sin might be brought to nothing, so that we would no longer be enslaved to sin" (Rom. 6:6 ESV), for we have "been set free from sin" (Rom. 6:18 ESV). And we are henceforth to count ourselves "dead to sin and alive to God in Christ Jesus" (Rom. 6:11 ESV).

The Bible also tells us that holiness is "perfect love," a love which must expel from the heart all hatred and every evil disposition contrary to love, just as you must first empty a cup of all oil that may be in it before you can fill it with water.

Thus, holiness is a state in which there is no anger, malice, blasphemy, hypocrisy, envy, love of ease, selfish desire for good opinion of others, shame of the cross, worldliness, deceit, debate, contention, covetousness, nor any evil desire or tendency in the heart.

It is a state in which there is no longer any doubt or fear.

It is a state in which God is loved and trusted with a perfect heart.

But though the heart may be perfect, the head may be very imperfect, and through such imperfections of memory, judgment, or reason, the holy man or woman may make many mistakes. But God looks at the sincerity of that person's purpose, at the love and faith of the heart rather than the imperfections of the head, and calls him or her holy.

Holiness is not absolute perfection, which belongs to God only. Nor is it angelic perfection. Nor is it Adamic perfection for, no doubt, Adam had a perfect head as well as a perfect heart before he sinned against God. But it is Christian perfection—such perfection and obedience of the heart as a poor fallen creature, aided by almighty power and boundless grace, can give.

It is that state of heart and life which consists of being and doing all the time—not by fits and starts, but steadily—just what God wants us to be and do.

Jesus said, "Make the tree good and its fruit good" (Matt. 12:33 ESV). Now, an apple tree is an apple tree all the time and can bring forth nothing but apples. So holiness is that perfect renewal of our nature that makes us essentially good, so that we continually bring forth fruit unto God—"the fruit of the Spirit [which] is love, joy, peace, patience, kindness, goodness, faithfulness, gentleness, [and] self-control" (Gal. 5:22–23 ESV)—with never a single work of the flesh grafted in among this heavenly fruit.

It is possible, right down here, where sin and Satan have once ruined us, for the Son of God thus to transform us, by enabling us to "put off the old self" with its deceitful desires and to "put on the new self, created after the likeness of God in true righteousness and holiness" (Eph. 4:22, 24 ESV), being "renewed in knowledge after the image of its creator" (Col. 3:10 ESV).

But someone may object: "Yes, all you say is true, but I don't believe we can be holy until the hour of death. The Christian life is a war, and we must fight the good fight of faith until we die. And *then* I believe God will give us dying grace."

Many honest Christians hold exactly this view and put forth no real effort to "stand firm in all the will of God, mature and fully assured" (Col. 4:12 NIV). And though they pray daily for God's kingdom to come and His will to be done on earth as it is in heaven (see Matt. 6:10), they do not believe it is possible for them to do the will of God, and so they make Jesus the author of a vain prayer, which is idle mockery to repeat.

But it is as easy for me to be and to do what God wants in this life every day as it is for the archangel Gabriel to be and do what God wants of him. If this is not the case, then God is neither good nor just in His requirements of me. God requires me to love and serve Him with all my heart, and Gabriel can do no more than that. And by God's grace, it is as easy for me as for the archangel.

Besides, God promises that if we return to the Lord and obey His commands with all our heart and soul, that He will circumcise our hearts that we may love Him with heart and soul (see Deut. 30:2, 6). And He promises "to rescue us from the hand of our enemies, and to enable us to serve him without fear in holiness and righteousness before him all our days" (Luke 1:74–75 NIV). This promise in itself ought to convince any honest soul that God means for us to be holy in this life.

The good fight of faith is a fight to retain this blessing against the assaults of Satan, the fogs of doubt, and the attacks of an ignorant and unbelieving church and world.

It is not a fight against ourselves after we are sanctified, for Paul expressly declared that "our struggle is not against flesh and blood, but against the rulers, against the authorities, against the powers of this dark world and against the spiritual forces of evil in the heavenly realms" (Eph. 6:12 NIV).

In the whole Word of God, there is not one sentence to prove that this blessing is not received before death. And surely it is only by accepting from God's hands His offered living grace that we can hope to be granted dying grace.

But the Bible declares that "God is able to make all grace abound to you, so that having all sufficiency in all things at all times, you may abound in every good work" (2 Cor. 9:8 ESV)—not at death, but in this life, when grace is needed and where our good works are to be done.

Holiness—How to Get It

2

A man more than eighty years old once said, "I believe in holiness, but I don't think it is all got at once, as you people say. I believe we grow into it."

This is a common mistake, second only to that which makes death the savior from sin and the giver of holiness, and it is a mistake which has kept tens of thousands out of the blessed experience. It does not recognize the exceeding sinfulness of sin (see Rom. 7:13), nor does it know the simple way of faith by which alone sin can be destroyed.

Entire sanctification is at once a process of subtraction and addition.

First, there are laid aside "all malice and all deceit and hypocrisy and envy and all slander" (1 Pet. 2:1 ESV)—in fact, every evil inclination and selfish desire that is unlike Christ—and the soul is cleansed. This cannot be by growth, for this cleansing takes something from the soul, while growth always adds something to it. The Bible says, "Put off all these: anger, wrath, malice, blasphemy, filthy language out of your mouth" (Col. 3:8 NKJV). The apostle Paul, who penned those words, talked as though we were to put these off in much the same way as we would a coat. It is not by growth that a person puts off a coat, but by an active, voluntary, and immediate effort of the whole body. This is subtraction.

But the apostle added: "Clothe yourselves with compassion, kindness, humility, gentleness and patience" (Col. 3:12 NIV). Neither does a person put on clothing by growth, but by a similar effort of the whole body.

You may grow *in* your coat, but not *into* your coat; you must first get it on. Just so, we may grow in grace, but not into grace. We may swim in water, but not into water.

It is not by growth that you get the weeds out of your garden, but by pulling them up and vigorously using your hoe and rake. It is not by growth that you expect that dirty little boy, who has been tumbling around with the dog and cat in the backyard, to get clean. He might grow to manhood and get dirtier every day. It is by washing with much pure water that you expect to make him at all presentable. So the Bible speaks of "him that loved us, and washed us from our sins in his own blood" (Rev. 1:5 KJV), saying, "the blood of Jesus, his Son, cleanses us from all sin" (1 John 1:7 NLT).

And it is just this we sing about:

> To get this blest washing I all things forgo;
> Now wash me, and I shall be whiter than snow.[1]

There is a fountain filled with blood

Drawn from Immanuel's veins,

And sinners plunged beneath its flood

Lose all their guilty stains.[2]

These facts were told to the old brother mentioned above, and he was asked if, after sixty years of Christian experience, he felt any nearer to the priceless gift of a clean heart than when he first began to serve Christ. He honestly confessed that he did not. He was asked next if he thought sixty years was long enough to prove the growth theory, if it were true. He thought it was, and so was asked to come forward and seek the blessing at once.

He did so, but did not win through that night. But the next night he came forward again and had scarcely knelt five minutes before he stood up and, stretching out his arms, while tears ran down his cheeks and his face glowed with heaven's light, he cried out, "As far as the east is from the west, so far has He removed [my] transgressions from [me]" (Ps. 103:12 NKJV). For some time after, he lived to witness to this wondrous grace of God in Christ.

"But," a man said to me, as I urged him to seek holiness at once, "I got this when I was converted. God didn't do a half work with me when He saved me. He did a thorough job."

I answered, "True, God did a thorough work, brother. When He gave you new life in Jesus Christ, He forgave all your sins, every one of them. He did not leave half of them unforgiven, but blotted out all of them, to be forgotten forever. He also adopted you into His family and sent His Holy Spirit into your heart to tell you that blessed bit of heavenly news. And that information made you feel happier than to have been told that you had fallen heir to a million dollars or been elected governor of a state, for this made you an heir of God and a joint heir of all things with our Lord and Savior Jesus Christ. It is a great thing. But, brother, are you saved from all impatience, anger, and like sins of the heart? Do you live a holy life?"

"Well, you see," the man said, "I don't look at this matter exactly as you do. I do not believe we can be saved from all impatience and anger in this life." And so, when pressed to the point, he begged the question and contradicted his own assertion that he had received holiness when he experienced new life in Christ. As a friend wrote, he "would rather deny the sickness than take the medicine."[3]

The fact is, neither the Bible nor experience proves that we get a clean heart when we enter the kingdom, but just the opposite. Our sins are forgiven. We receive the witness of adoption into God's own family. Our affections are changed. But before we go very far we find our patience mixed up with some degree of impatience, our kindness with wrath, our meekness with anger, our humility with pride, our loyalty to Jesus mixed with a shame of the cross, and, in fact, the fruit of the Spirit all mixed up together with the works of the flesh, in greater or lesser degree.

But this will be done away with when we get a clean heart, and it will take a second work of grace, preceded by a wholehearted consecration and as definite an act of faith to get it as that which preceded conversion.

After conversion, we find our old sinful nature much like a tree that has been cut down, but the stump still left. The tree causes no more bother, but the stump will still bring forth little shoots if it is not watched. The quickest and most effective way is to put some dynamite under the stump and blow it up.

Just so, God wants to put the dynamite of the Holy Spirit (the word *dynamite* comes from the Greek word for power, in Acts 1:8) into every follower of Jesus and forever do away with that old troublesome, sinful nature, so that he or she can truly say, "Old things are passed away; behold, all things are become new" (2 Cor. 5:17 KJV). This is just what God did with the apostles on the day of Pentecost. Nobody will deny that they were followers of Jesus before Pentecost, for Jesus Himself had told them to "rejoice, because your names are written in heaven" (Luke 10:20 KJV), and a person must be a true follower of Jesus before his or her name is written in heaven.

And again Jesus said of His earliest followers, "They are not of the world, even as I am not of the world" (John 17:16 KJV), and this could not be said of the unregenerate. So we may conclude that they had entered the kingdom of God, yet did not have the blessing of a clean heart until the day of Pentecost.

That they did receive it there, Peter declared about as plainly as possible when he said, later, "God, who knows the heart, showed that he accepted them by giving the Holy Spirit to them, just as he did to us. He did not discriminate between us and them, for he purified their hearts by faith" (Acts 15:8–9 NIV).

Before Peter got this great blessing he was filled with presumption one day and fear the next. One day he told Jesus, "Even if all fall away on account of you, I never will. . . . Even if I have to die with you, I will never disown you" (Matt. 26:33, 35 NIV). And shortly after, when the mob came to arrest his Master, he boldly attacked them with a sword; but a few hours later, when his blood had cooled and the excitement was over, he was so frightened by a maid that he cursed and swore and denied his Master three times.

He was like a good many folks, who are tremendously brave when trumpets blow and the winds are favorable—and who can even stand an attack from persecutors, where muscle and physical courage can come to the front—but who have no moral courage when they have to face the scorn of their colleagues and the jeers of strangers. These are soldiers who love dress parade, but do not want hard fighting at the front of the battle.

But Peter got over that on the day of Pentecost. He received the power of the Holy Spirit coming into him. He obtained a clean heart, from which perfect love had cast out all fear. And then, when shut in prison for preaching on the street and commanded by the supreme court of the land not to do so any more, he answered, "Whether it's right in God's sight to listen to you rather than to God, you must judge; for we cannot keep from speaking about what we have seen and heard" (Acts 4:19–20 NRSV). And then, just as soon as he was released, into the street he went again to preach the good news of salvation "to the uttermost" (Heb. 7:25 KJV).

You could not scare Peter after that, nor could he be lifted up with spiritual pride. For one day, after God used him to heal a lame man and "all the people were astonished and came running," Peter saw it and said, "Fellow Israelites, why does this surprise you? Why do you stare at us as if by our own power or godliness we had made this man walk? The God . . . of our fathers, has glorified his servant Jesus. . . .

By faith in the name of Jesus, this man whom you see and know was made strong. It is Jesus' name and the faith that comes through him that has completely healed him" (Acts 3:12–13, 16 NIV).

Nor did Peter have any of that ugly temper he showed when he cut off that poor fellow's ear the night Jesus was arrested, but armed himself with the mind that was in Christ (see 1 Pet. 4:1) and followed Him who left us an example that we should follow His steps.

"But we cannot have what Peter obtained on the day of Pentecost," wrote someone to me recently. However, Peter himself, in that great sermon which he preached that day, declared that we can, for he said, "You will receive the gift of the Holy Spirit. The promise is for you and your children and for all who are far off"—nineteen hundred years from now—"for all whom the Lord our God will call" (Acts 2:38–39 NIV).

Any child of God can have this. You must give yourself wholly to God and ask for it in faith. "Ask, and it will be given to you; seek, and you will find. . . . If you then, who are evil, know how to give good gifts to your children, how much more will the heavenly Father give the Holy Spirit to those who ask him!" (Luke 11:9, 13 ESV).

Seek Him with all your heart, and you shall find Him. You shall indeed, for God says so, and He is waiting to give Himself to you.

A dear young fellow, a candidate for Salvation Army ministry, felt his need of a clean heart. He went home from the holiness meeting,[4] took his Bible, knelt down by his bed, read the second chapter of Acts, and then told the Lord that he would not get up from his knees till he got a clean heart, full of the Holy Spirit. He had not prayed long before the Lord came suddenly to him and filled him with the glory of God. And his face did shine, and his testimony did burn in people's hearts after that!

You can have it, if you will go to the Lord in the Spirit and with the faith of that brother. And the Lord will do for you "immeasurably more than all [you] ask or imagine, according to the power that is at work within [you]" (Eph. 3:20 NIV).

NOTES

1. James L. Nicholson, "Whiter Than Snow," 1872, public domain.

2. William Cowper, "There Is a Fountain Filled with Blood," 1772, public domain.

3. The source for this quote is unknown.

4. *Holiness meeting* in The Salvation Army has been the name for the Sunday morning or sometimes Friday night worship service when traditionally the doctrine of holiness and exhortation to holy living has taken place.

Hindrances to Obtaining the Blessing

Holiness does not have legs and does not walk around, visiting idle people, as one Christian seemed to think who told me that he thought the experience would come to him someday. A Christian sister aptly remarked, "He might as well expect the church building to come to him."

The fact is, there are hindrances in the way of holiness with most people. But you who seek the experience must put from you forever the thought that any of these hindrances are in God, or in your circumstances, for they are not, but are altogether in yourselves. This being true, it is extreme folly to sit down with indifference and quietly wait with folded hands for the blessed experience to come to you. Be sure of this: it will not come, any more than a crop of potatoes will come to the lazy fellow who sits in the shade and never lifts his hoe, nor does a stroke of labor through all the spring and summer months. The rule in the spiritual world is this: "If you don't work, you don't eat" (2 Thess. 3:10 CEV) and "You will harvest what you plant" (Gal. 6:7 CEV).

Therefore, the way of wisdom is to begin at once—by a diligent study of God's Word, much secret prayer, unflinching self-examination, rigid self-denial, hearty obedience to all present light, and a faithful attendance at the meetings of God's people—to find out what these hindrances are, and by the grace of God to put them away, though it cost as much pain as to cut off a right hand or to pluck out a right eye.

The Bible tells us—and the testimony and experience of all holy people agree—that one great practical hindrance to holiness is imperfect consecration.

Before a watchmaker can clean and regulate my watch, I must give it unreservedly into his hands. Before a doctor can cure me, I must take her medicine in the manner and at the time she requires. Before a captain can navigate me across the trackless ocean, I must get on board his ship and stay there. Just so, if I would have God cleanse and regulate my heart with all its affections, if I would have Him cure my sin-sick soul, if I would have Him take me safely across the ocean of time into that greater ocean of eternity, I must put myself fully into His hands and stay there. I must be perfectly consecrated to Him.

A Salvation Army captain knelt with her soldiers, and sang: "Anywhere with Jesus I will go," adding: "Anywhere but to h____, Lord." Her consecration was imperfect, and today she is out of Salvation Army work. There were some things she would not do for Jesus, and therefore Jesus would not cleanse or keep her.

The other day, a poor man who had strayed from God told me that he knew, at one time, that he ought to give up tobacco. God wanted him to do so, but he held on to it and used it secretly. His imperfect consecration kept him from holiness and led to his downfall, and today he walks the streets as a common drunkard, on the open road to hell. In his heart was secret disloyalty, and God could not cleanse or keep him. God wants perfect loyalty in the secret of your own heart, and He demands it, not only for His glory, but also for your good—for, if you can understand it, God's highest glory and your highest good are one and the same thing.

This consecration consists in a perfect putting off of your own will, disposition, temper, desires, likes, dislikes, and a perfect putting on of Christ's will, disposition, temper, desires, likes, and dislikes. In short, perfect consecration is giving up your own will in all things and receiving Jesus' will instead. This may seem impossible and disagreeable to your unsanctified heart. But if you mean business for eternity, and will intelligently and unflinchingly look at this strict gate through which so few enter, and tell the Lord that you want to go through that way though it cost you your life, the Holy Spirit will soon show you that it is not only possible but easy and delightful thus to yield yourself to God.

The second hindrance in the way of the person who would be holy is imperfect faith. When Paul wrote to the church in Thessalonica, he praised them for being "an example to all the believers in Macedonia and in Achaia," and added, "your faith in God has gone forth everywhere" (1 Thess. 1:7–8 ESV). That was the best believing church in all Europe, and so real and sturdy was their faith that they could endure much persecution. But their faith was not perfect, for Paul added, "We pray most earnestly night and day that we may see you face to face and supply what is lacking in your faith" (1 Thess. 3:10 ESV). And because of their imperfect faith they were not sanctified; so we find the apostle prayed, "May the God of peace himself sanctify you completely" (1 Thess. 5:23 ESV).

All who are born of God and have the witness of His Spirit to their justification know full well that it was not through any good works of their own, nor by growing into it, that they were saved, but it was "by grace . . . through faith" (Eph. 2:8 KJV). But very many of these dear people seem to think that we are to grow into sanctification, or are to get it by our own works. But the Lord settled that question, and made it as plain as words can make it, when He told Paul that He sent him to the Gentiles to "open their eyes, so that they may turn from darkness to light and from the power of Satan to God, that they may receive forgiveness of sins and a place among those who are sanctified by faith in me" (Acts 26:18 ESV). Not by works, nor by growth, but by faith were they to be made holy.

If you will be holy you must come to God "with a true heart in full assurance of faith" (Heb. 10:22 ESV), and then, if you will wait patiently before Him, the wonderwork shall be done.

Consecration and faith are matters of the heart, and the trouble with most people is there. But some people's trouble is with the head. They fail to get the blessing because they seek something altogether too small.

Holiness is a great blessing. It is the renewal of the whole heart and life in the image of Jesus. It is the utter destruction of all hatred, envy, malice, impatience, covetousness, pride, lust, love of ease, love of human admiration and applause, love of splendor, shame of the cross, self-will, and the like. It makes its possessors "gentle and lowly in heart" (Matt. 11:29 ESV), as Jesus was, as well as patient, kind, full of compassion and love, full of faith, benevolent, and zealous in every good word and work.

I have heard some people claim the blessing of holiness because they had given up tobacco or something of that sort while they were still impatient, unkind, or absorbed with the cares of this life. Thus, they soon got discouraged, concluded there was no such blessing, and became bitter opponents of the doctrine of holiness. Their trouble was in seeking too small a blessing. They gave up certain outward things, but the inward self-life was still uncrucified. The gold miner washes the dirt off his ore, but he cannot wash the dross out of it. The fire must do that, and then the gold will be pure. So the laying aside of outward things is necessary, but only the baptism of the Holy Spirit and of fire can purify the secret desires and affections of the heart and make it holy. And this you must earnestly seek by perfect consecration and perfect faith.

Other people fail to obtain the blessing because they seek something altogether distinct from holiness. They want a vision of heaven, of balls of fire, of some angel. Or they want an experience that will save them from all trials and temptations and from all possible mistakes and infirmities. Or they want a power that will make sinners fall as if dead when they speak.

They overlook the verse that declares, "The purpose of the commandment is love from a pure heart, from a good conscience, and from sincere faith" (1 Tim. 1:5 NKJV). That verse teaches us that holiness is nothing more than a pure heart filled with perfect love, a clear conscience toward God and others, which comes from a faithful discharge of duty and simple faith without any hypocrisy. They overlook the fact that purity and perfect love are so Christlike and so rare in this world, that they are in themselves a great, great blessing.

They overlook the fact that while Jesus was a great man, King of Kings and Lord of Lords, He was also a lowly carpenter and "emptied himself by taking the form of a slave and . . . humbled himself" (Phil. 2:7–8 CEB). They overlook the fact that they are to be—as Jesus was— "in this present world," and that "this present world" is the place of His humiliation, where He is "despised and rejected," a "man of sorrows, acquainted with deepest grief," with "nothing beautiful or majestic about his appearance, nothing to attract us to him" (Isa. 53:2–3 NLT). His only beauty in "this present world" is that inward "beauty of holiness" (1 Chron. 16:29 KJV), that humble spirit of gentleness and love, "the unfading beauty of a gentle and quiet spirit, which is so precious to God" (1 Pet. 3:4 NLT).

Is your soul hungering and thirsting for the righteousness of perfect love? Do you want to be like Jesus? Are you prepared to suffer with Him and to be hated by all for His name's sake? Then, "lay aside every weight, and the sin which so easily ensnares" you (Heb. 12:1 NKJV), present your body "a living sacrifice, holy, acceptable unto God, which is your reasonable service" (Rom. 12:1 KJV), and "run with patience the race that is set before [you], looking unto Jesus the author and finisher of [your] faith" (Heb. 12:1–2 KJV). If you will then resist all Satan's temptations to doubt, you will soon find all your hindrances gone, and yourself rejoicing "with joy inexpressible and full of glory" (1 Pet. 1:8 NKJV).

"Now may the God of peace make you holy in every way, and may your whole spirit and soul and body be kept blameless until our Lord Jesus Christ comes again. God will make this happen, for he who calls you is faithful" (1 Thess. 5:23–24 NLT).

The Temptations of the Sanctified

4

"How can someone who is dead to sin be tempted?" an earnest but unsanctified Christian asked me some time ago. If the very tendencies and inclinations to sin are destroyed, what is there in the person to respond to a solicitation to evil?

Everyone asks this question sooner or later, and when God showed me the answer, it threw great light on my pathway and helped me to defeat Satan in many a pitched battle.

The truly sanctified believer who is dead to sin does not have any inclinations remaining that respond to ordinary temptations. As Paul declared, "We wrestle not against flesh and blood"—against the sensual, fleshly, and worldly temptations which used to have such power over us—"but against principalities, against powers, against the rulers of the darkness of this world, against spiritual wickedness in high places" (Eph. 6:12 KJV).

If he were once a drinking man, he is no longer tempted in the least to get drunk, for he has "died" and his life "is hidden with Christ in God" (Col. 3:3 NLT). If she were ever proud and vain, delighting in dress and jewels, she is no longer allured by the cheap glitter and the vain pomp and glory of this world, for she has set her affection on things above, not on things on the earth (see Col. 3:2). If they once coveted the honor and praise of others, they now count such as dung and dross, that they may win Christ and have the honor that comes from God only. If they once desired riches and ease, they now gladly give up all earthly possessions and comforts that they may have treasure in heaven; they do not get "tied up with civilian matters, so that they can please the one who recruited them" (2 Tim. 2:4 CEB). Such things now have no more attraction for the sanctified heart than the baubles and trinkets of childhood.

I do not mean to say that Satan will never hold up any of these worldly and fleshly pleasures and honors to induce the soul to leave Christ, for he will. But I do mean to say that the soul being now dead to sin—having the very roots of sin destroyed—does not respond to the suggestion of Satan, but instantly rejects it. Satan may send along a beautiful adulteress, as he did to Joseph in Egypt, but the sanctified person will flee away and cry out, as Joseph did, "How could I do this terrible thing and sin against God?" (Gen. 39:9 CEB).

Or Satan may offer great power and honor and riches, as he did to Moses in Egypt, but comparing these with the infinite fullness of glory and power that are found in Christ, the sanctified heart will instantly reject the Devil's offer, "choosing rather to endure ill treatment with the people of God than to enjoy the passing pleasures of sin, considering the reproach of Christ greater riches than the treasures of Egypt" (Heb. 11:25–26 NASB).

Or again, Satan may tempt the sanctified person's palate with the dainty wines and rich delicacies of a king's palace, as he did Daniel in Babylon. But like Daniel, he or she will choose discipline and obedience over indulgence (see Dan. 1:8).

All these worldly baits were held out to Jesus (see Matt. 4:1–11; Luke 4:2–13), but we see in the biblical account how gloriously He triumphed over every suggestion of the Tempter. And just as He rejected Satan's temptations and gained the victory, so will sanctified men and women, for they have Christ Himself dwelling in their hearts and fighting their battles, and they can now say with the Master, "the ruler of the world is coming, and he has nothing in Me" (John 14:30 NASB).

Those who have died to sin have found such satisfaction, peace, joy, comfort, purity, and power in Christ that the power of temptation along any of the old lines is completely broken, and they now enjoy the liberty of the sons and daughters of God. They are as free as any archangel, for "if the Son sets you free, you are truly free" (John 8:36 NLT), even with "the liberty by which Christ has made us free" (Gal. 5:1 NKJV).

But while Christ has set the sanctified man or woman at liberty, and the fight against the old worldly passions and fleshly appetites is a thing of the past, a continual warfare with Satan to keep this liberty remains. This warfare is what Paul called "the good fight of faith" (1 Tim. 6:12 KJV).

The sanctified believer must fight to hold fast his or her faith in the Savior's blood, in the Spirit's sanctifying power. Although not seen by the world, this fight is as real as that of Waterloo or Gettysburg, and its far-reaching consequences for good or evil are infinitely greater.

⚊ By faith, we who are sanctified become heirs of God with Jesus Christ (see Rom. 8:17), and our faith makes this heavenly inheritance so real to us that the influence of unseen things far surpasses the influence of the things we see, hear, and handle. We say with Paul, and fully realize it in our hearts as we say it, that "the things that are seen are transient, but the things that are unseen are eternal" (2 Cor. 4:18 ESV) and will remain when "the elements shall melt with fervent heat" (2 Pet. 3:10 KJV), and "the skies roll up like a scroll" (Isa. 34:4 ESV).

These things can only be held by faith. But so long as we thus hold them, Satan's power over us is utterly broken. This the Devil knows quite well, so he begins systematic warfare against the faith of such a person.

He will accuse us of sin, when our conscience is as clear of willfully breaking God's law as is the conscience of an angel. But Satan knows that if he can get us to listen to his accusations and lose faith in the cleansing blood of Jesus, he has us at his mercy. Satan, "the accuser of our brothers and sisters" (Rev. 12:10 NLT), will then turn right around and declare that it is the Holy Spirit, instead of himself, condemning us! Here is the difference we want to notice: the Devil accuses us of sin; the Holy Spirit convicts us of sin. If I break any of God's commandments, the Holy Spirit will convict me at once. Satan will accuse me of having sinned when I have not, and he cannot prove it.

For instance, a sanctified person talks to others about their souls and urges them to give their hearts to God, but they do not. Then Satan begins to accuse the Christian: "You did not say the right things; if you had, they would have given in to God."

It is no use arguing with the Devil. The Christian can only look to the Savior and say, "Dear Lord, you know I have done the best I could. If I have done anything wrong or left anything undone, I trust Your blood to cleanse me."

If we meet Satan this way at the beginning of his accusation, our faith will gain a victory and we will rejoice in the Savior's cleansing blood and the Spirit's keeping power. But if we listen to the Devil until our conscience and faith are both wounded, it may take a long time for our faith to regain the strength that will enable us to shout and triumph over all the power of the Enemy.

When Satan has injured the faith of the sanctified individual, he will begin to blacken God's character. He will suggest to that person that the Father no longer loves him or her with that mighty love He had for His Son, Jesus; yet Jesus declares that He does. Then Satan will suggest that, maybe, the blood does not cleanse from all sin and that the Holy Spirit cannot—or at least, does not—keep anybody spotless and blameless, and that, after all, there is no such thing as a holy life down here in this world.

As a further result of this wounded faith, that person's secret prayer loses much of its blessedness; a formerly intense desire to speak to others about spiritual things will grow dull; the joy of witnessing for Christ will grow less, and dry talk will take the place of burning testimony; and the Bible will cease to be a constant source of blessing and strength. Then the Devil will tempt that soul to actual sin, through the neglect of some of these duties.

Now if that person listens to Satan and begins to doubt, does not cry mightily to God, does not search the Bible to know God's will and find His promises and plead them day and night, as Jesus did, "who in the days of his flesh . . . offered up prayers and supplications with strong crying and tears unto him that was able to save him from death" (Heb. 5:7 KJV), woe be to his or her faith! If that sanctified soul does not hurl these promises at Satan and resolutely shut his or her ears to every suggestion to doubt God, it is only a question of time until that person is numbered among those who have a reputation of life yet are dead (see Rev. 3:1), whose prayers and testimonies are lifeless, whose Bible study and exhortations and works are dead because there is no living faith in them, "having a form of godliness but denying its power" (2 Tim. 3:5 NIV), and perhaps in time even turning from the faith altogether.

What shall the sanctified person do to overcome the Devil? Listen to what Peter said: "Be sober-minded; be watchful. Your adversary the devil prowls around like a roaring lion, seeking someone to devour. Resist him, firm in your faith" (1 Pet. 5:8–9 ESV).

Hear James: "Resist the devil, and he will flee from you" (James 4:7 NLT).

Listen to Paul: "Fight the good fight of faith" (1 Tim. 6:12 KJV). "The righteous shall live by faith" (Rom. 1:17 ESV). Take "the shield of faith with which you will be able to quench all the fiery darts of the wicked one" (Eph. 6:16 NKJV).

And John: "This is the victory that has overcome the world—our faith" (1 John 5:4 ESV). "And they overcame him," (the Devil, the accuser), "by the blood of the Lamb, and by the word of their testimony; and they loved not their lives unto the death" (Rev. 12:11 KJV). They obeyed God at all costs and denied themselves to the uttermost.

And the author of Hebrews attached the same importance to testimony when saying: "Let us hold fast the confession of our hope without wavering" (Heb. 10:23 ESV).

"Take care, brothers and sisters, that none of you may have an evil, unbelieving heart that turns away from the living God" (Heb. 3:12 NRSV) and "do not throw away this confident trust in the LORD. Remember the great reward it brings you!" (Heb. 10:35 NLT).

After the Holiness Meeting 5

Did you come forward to the penitent form[1] at the holiness meeting? Did Jesus make your heart clean? Did you receive the Holy Spirit?

If you gave yourself to God in the very best way you knew but did not receive the Holy Spirit, I beg you not to be discouraged. Do not take a backward step. Stand where you are, and hold fast to your faith. The Lord means to bless you. Keep looking to Jesus, and fully expect Him to satisfy your heart's desire. Tell Him you expect it, and plead His promises. He said, "For I know the plans I have for you. . . . They are plans for good and not for disaster, to give you a future and a hope. In those days when you pray, I will listen. If you look for me wholeheartedly, you will find me. I will be found by you" (Jer. 29:11–14 NLT). This is a wonderful promise, and it is for you.

Has the Devil tempted you, more than ever, since then? Well, here is another promise for you: "Suffering one, storm-tossed, uncomforted,

look, I am setting your gemstones in silvery metal and your foundations
with sapphires. I will make your towers of rubies, and your gates of beryl,
and all your walls of precious jewels. . . . You will be firmly founded
in righteousness" (Isa. 54:11–12, 14 CEB).

God is going to do wonderful things for you, if you will not cast
away your faith and your boldness.

Remember, you not only gave yourself to God, but God gave Himself
to you. You did receive the Holy Spirit. When He came in, self went out.
You abhorred—loathed—yourself, and sank into nothingness, while Jesus
became all and in all. That is the first thing the Holy Spirit does when He
comes into the heart in all His fullness—He glorifies Jesus. We see Jesus
as we never saw Him before. We love Him. We adore Him. We ascribe
all honor and glory and power to Him, and we realize, as we never did
before, that through His precious blood we are saved and sanctified.

The Holy Spirit will not call attention to Himself, but will point to
Jesus (see John 15:26; 16:13–14). Nor does He come to reveal any new
truth, but rather to make us understand the old. "He will teach you all
things and bring to your remembrance all that I have said to you" (John
14:26 ESV). He will make your Bible a new book to you. He will teach you
how to apply it to everyday life, so that you will be safely guided by it.

The reason people get mixed up over the Bible is because they do
not have the Holy Spirit. A young Christian full of the Holy Spirit can
tell more about the Bible than all the doctors of divinity and theological professors in the world who are not filled with the Holy Spirit. The
Holy Spirit will make you love your Bible, and you will say with Job,
"I have treasured the words of His mouth more than my necessary food"
(Job 23:12 NASB), and with the psalmist you will declare His judgments

to be "sweeter also than honey and the honeycomb" (Ps. 19:10 KJV).
No book or paper can take its place; but, like the blessed person of
Psalm 1, you will "meditate [therein] day and night" (Ps. 1:2 KJV; see
also Josh. 1:8). The Holy Spirit will make you tremble at the warnings
of God's Word (see Isa. 66:2), exult in God's promises, and take delight
in the commandments. You will say with Jesus, "No one can live only
on food. People need every word that God has spoken" (Matt. 4:4 CEV).
You will understand what Jesus meant when He said, "The words that
I have spoken to you are spirit and life" (John 6:63 ESV).

While you walk in humble obedience and childlike faith, trusting in
the blood of Jesus to cleanse you from all sin, the Comforter will abide
with you, and the "low water mark" of your experience will be perfect
peace. I will not dare to say what the high water mark may be! Like
Paul, you may get "caught up to the third [heaven]" at times and hear
"things so astounding that they cannot be expressed in words, things
no human is allowed to tell" (2 Cor. 12:4 NLT). Oh, there are unspeakable breadths, lengths, depths, and heights of the love of God for you
to revel in and discover by the telescope and microscope of faith! You
need not fear that the experience will wear out or grow tame. God is
infinite, and your little mind and heart cannot exhaust the wonders of
His wisdom and goodness and grace and glory in one short lifetime.

Do not think, however, when the tide flows out to the low water
mark that the Comforter has left you. I remember well how, after I
had received the Holy Spirit, I walked for weeks under a weight of
divine joy and glory that was almost too much for my body to bear.
Then the joy began to subside, and there would be alternate days of
joy and peace. And on the days when there was no special experience,

the Devil would tempt me with the thought that I had in some way grieved the Holy Spirit and that He was leaving me. But God taught me that it was the Devil's lie, and I must "hold fast the profession of [my] faith without wavering" (Heb. 10:23 KJV). So I say to you, do not think that just because you are not overflowing with emotion it means He has left you. Hold fast to your faith. He is with you. After the great trouble He went through to get into your heart, He will not leave you without first letting you know just why He goes. The Holy Spirit is not capricious and fickle. He has to strive long to get into your heart, and He will strive long before He will leave it, unless you willfully harden your heart and drive Him from you.

I am not writing this, however, for those who are careless and would as soon grieve Him as not, but for you whose heart is tender, who love Him and would rather die than lose Him out of your heart. I say to you, trust Him! When I had almost yielded to Satan's lie that the Lord had left me, God gave me this text: "The people of Israel argued with Moses and tested the LORD by saying, 'Is the LORD here with us or not?'" (Ex. 17:7 NLT).

I saw that to doubt God's presence with me, even though I felt no special sign of His presence, was to tempt Him. So I promised the Lord then that I would not doubt, but would be strong in faith. He has not left me yet, and I am persuaded He never will. I can trust my wife when I cannot see her, and so I have learned to trust my Lord, even if I do not always feel the same mighty stirrings of His power in me. I tell Him that I trust Him, I believe He is with me, and I will not please the Devil by doubting.

Just at this stage, after having received the Holy Spirit, many people get confused. In time of temptation they think the Spirit has left them, and instead of trusting and acknowledging His presence and thanking Him for stooping so low as to dwell in their poor hearts, they begin to seek Him as though He had not already come, or as if He had gone away. They should stop seeking at once and start fighting the Devil by faith, telling him to get behind them, and go on praising the Lord for His presence with them. If you will seek light when you have light, you will find darkness and confusion. If you begin to seek the Holy Spirit when you already have Him, you will grieve Him. What He wants is that you have faith. Therefore, having received Him into your hearts, continually acknowledge His presence, obey Him, glory in Him, and He will abide with you forever, and His presence will be powerful in you.

Do not keep seeking and crying for more power. Rather, seek by prayer and watchfulness, the study of your Bible, and the honest improvement of every opportunity to be a perfectly free channel for the power of the Holy Spirit, who is now in you. Believe God and do not obstruct the way of the Holy Spirit, that He may work through you. Ask Him to teach and guide you, that you may not hinder Him in His work. Seek to think His thoughts, speak His words, feel His love, and exercise His faith. Seek to be so guided by Him that you will pray when He wants you to pray, sing when He wants you to sing, and last but not least be silent when He wants you to be silent. "Live in the Spirit . . . walk in the Spirit" (Gal. 5:25 KJV) and "be filled with the Spirit" (Eph. 5:18 KJV).

Finally, do not be surprised if you have very unusual temptations. Remember that it was after Jesus was baptized with the Holy Spirit that he was led into the wilderness to be tempted by the Devil for forty days and forty nights (see Matt. 3:16–17; 4:1–3). "Disciples are not better than their teacher" (Matt. 10:24 CEV). But when you are tempted, "count it all joy" (James 1:2 KJV). Your very trials and temptations will lead you into a deeper acquaintance with Jesus, for as He was, so are you to be in this present world. Remember He said, "My grace is sufficient for you" (2 Cor. 12:9 NIV), and it is written of Him: "Since he himself has gone through suffering and testing, he is able to help us when we are being tested" (Heb. 2:18 NLT). "For we do not have a high priest who is unable to empathize with our weaknesses, but we have one who has been tempted in every way, just as we are—yet he did not sin" (Heb. 4:15 NIV). So then, "What shall we then say to these things? If God be for us, who can be against us?" (Rom. 8:31 KJV).

Be true. Be full of faith, and you will be able to say with Paul, "In all these things we are more than conquerors through him that loved us. For I am persuaded, that neither death, nor life, nor angels, nor principalities, nor powers, nor things present, nor things to come, nor height, nor depth, nor any other creature, shall be able to separate us from the love of God, which is in Christ Jesus our Lord" (Rom. 8:37–39 KJV).

NOTE

1. The penitent form, also called the mercy seat, is a bench-like furnishing at the front of Salvation Army chapels. People are invited, usually at the conclusion of the meeting, to come, kneel, and pray about their spiritual needs.

Fight the Good Fight of Faith **6**

A friend with whom I once billeted claimed the blessing of a clean heart and testified to it at the breakfast table the next morning. He said he had doubted whether there was such an experience, but since going to The Salvation Army he had been led to study the Bible and observe the lives of those who professed the blessing, and he had come to the conclusion that he could not serve God acceptably without holiness of heart. The difficulty was to reach the point where he would take it by faith. He said he had expected to get it sometime, had hoped for it, and had looked forward to the time when he should be pure, but finally he saw that it must be claimed. And right there began his fight of faith. He took hold of one end of the promise, and the Devil got hold of the other end, and they pulled and fought for the victory.

The Devil had often gotten the victory before. This time the man would not cast away his confidence, but came "boldly unto the throne of grace" (Heb. 4:16 KJV). The Devil was conquered by faith, and the brother walked off with the blessing of a clean heart. That morning he said, "God filled me with the Spirit last night," while the glad tones of his voice and the bright light of his face backed up his words.

The last thing a soul has to give up, when seeking salvation or sanctification, is "an evil heart of unbelief" (Heb. 3:12 KJV). This is Satan's stronghold. You may drive him from all his outposts and he does not care much, but when you assail this citadel he will resist with all the lies and cunning he can command. He does not care much if people give up outward sin. A respectable sinner will suit his purpose quite as well as the most disreputable. In fact, I am not sure that some people are worse than the Devil wants them to be, for they are a bad advertisement for him. Nor does he care very much if people indulge a hope of salvation or of purity. Indeed, I suspect he likes them to do so, if he can get them to stop there. But let a poor soul say, "I want to know I am saved now. I must have the blessing now. I can't live any longer without the witness of the Spirit that Jesus saves me now, and cleanses me now," and the Devil will begin to roar and lie and use all his wits to deceive that soul and switch it onto some side track or rock it to sleep with a promise of victory at some future time.

This is where the Devil really begins. Many people who say they are fighting the Devil do not know what fighting the Devil means. It is a fight of faith in which the soul takes hold of the promise of God and holds on to it and believes it and declares it to be true in spite of all the Devil's lies—in spite of all circumstances and feelings to the contrary—and obeys God, whether God seems to be fulfilling the promise or not. When a soul gets to the point where he or she will do this, and will hold fast to the profession of faith without wavering, he or she will soon get out of the fogs and mists and twilight of doubt and uncertainty into the broad day of perfect assurance. Such a soul shall know that Jesus saves and sanctifies, and shall be filled with a humbling, yet unutterably joyful sense of God's everlasting love and favor.

A friend whom I love as my own soul sought the blessing of a clean heart and gave up everything but his "evil heart of unbelief"—but did not understand that he was still holding on to that. He waited for God to give him the blessing. The Devil whispered to him, "You say you are on the altar for God, but you don't feel any different." The "evil heart of unbelief" in the poor fellow's heart took the Devil's part and said, "That is so." So my friend felt all discouraged, and the Devil got the victory.

Again he gave himself up, after a hard struggle—all but the "evil heart of unbelief." Again the Devil whispered, "You say you are all the Lord's, but you do not feel as other folks say they felt when they yielded all to God." The "evil heart of unbelief" again said, "That's so," and again the man fell, through unbelief.

A third time, after much effort, he sought the blessing and gave God all but the "evil heart of unbelief." The third time the Devil whispered, "You say you are all the Lord's, but you know what a quick temper you have. Now, how do you know but what next week an unlooked-for temptation may come that will overthrow you?" Again the "evil heart of unbelief" said, "That's so," and for the third time my friend was beaten back from the prize.

But at last he became so desperate in his hunt for God and in his desire for holiness and the Spirit's witness that there and then he was willing for God to show him all the depravity of his soul. And God showed him that his "evil heart of unbelief" had been listening to the Devil's voice and taking the Devil's part all the time. Good people, professing Christians, do not like to admit that they have any unbelief remaining in them, but until they acknowledge all the evil that is in them and take God's part against themselves, He cannot sanctify them.

Again he came and put his all on the altar, and told God he would trust Him. Again the Devil whispered, "You don't feel any different," but this time the man hushed the evil spirit of unbelief and answered, "I do not care if I do not feel any different. I am all the Lord's."

"But you do not feel as other folks say they feel," whispered the Devil.

"I do not care if I do not. I am all the Lord's, and He can bless me or not, just as He pleases."

"But there is your quick temper."

"I do not care. I am the Lord's, and I will trust Him to manage my temper. I am the Lord's! I am the Lord's!"

And there he stood, resisting the Devil, "steadfast in the faith" (1 Pet. 5:9 NKJV), and refusing to listen to the suggestions of "an evil heart of unbelief" all that day and night and the following day. There was a stillness in his soul and a fixed determination to stand on the promises of God forever, whether God blessed him or not. About ten o'clock the second night, as he was getting ready to go to bed, without any unusual expectation or premonition, God fulfilled His ancient promise: "The Lord, whom you seek, will suddenly come to His temple" (Mal. 3:1 NKJV). Jesus, the Son of God, was revealed in him, and made known to his spiritual consciousness, until he was "lost in wonder, love and praise."[1] Oh, how he exulted and triumphed in God his Savior and rejoiced that he had held fast his faith and resisted the Devil!

Now, every soul that gets into the kingdom of God must come to this point. The soul must die to sin, renounce all unbelief, and give up all doubts. He or she must consent to be "crucified with Christ" (Gal. 2:20 KJV) now. When this is done, that soul will touch God, feel the fire of His love, and be filled with His power, as surely as an electric streetcar receives power when proper connection is made with the wire above.

May God help you to see that now is "just the right time" (2 Cor. 6:2 NLT). Remember, if you are all given up to God, everything that makes you doubt is from Satan and not from God, and God commands you to "resist the devil and stay strong in your faith" (1 Pet. 5:9 CEV); "do not cast away your confidence, which has great reward" (Heb. 10:35 NKJV).

NOTE

1. Charles Wesley, "Love Divine, All Loves Excelling," 1747, public domain.

The Heart of Jesus 7

We sang the following verse with all our might one morning when I was a cadet (student) in The Salvation Army training school:

> Give me a heart like Thine;
> By Thy wonderful power,
> By Thy grace every hour,
> Give me a heart like Thine.[1]

In one of those hours of heart humbling and heart searching, at least one of the cadets looked through the words and caught the spirit of the song. He came to me at the close of the meeting with a serious look and a tone of earnest inquiry and asked, "Do we really mean it, that we can have a heart like His?" I told him that I was certain we could and that the dear Lord wanted to give us hearts just like His own—

A humble, lowly, contrite heart,

Believing, true, and clean.

A heart in every thought renewed,

And full of love Divine;

Perfect and right and pure and good,

A copy, Lord, of Thine.[2]

Indeed, Jesus was "the firstborn among many brothers and sisters" (Rom. 8:29 NLT). He is our "elder brother" (see Heb. 2:10–11) and we are to be like Him. "As he is, so are we in this world" (1 John 4:17 KJV), and "Those who say they live in God should live their lives as Jesus did" (1 John 2:6 NLT). Now, it is impossible for us to walk like Him, to live like Him, unless we have a heart like His.

We cannot bear the same kind of fruit unless we are the same kind of tree. So Jesus wants to make us like Himself. We judge trees by their fruit, and so we judge Jesus, and then we can find out what kind of a heart He had. Let us judge and consider what His heart was.

We find love in Him; therefore Jesus had a loving heart. He bore the luscious fruit of perfect love. There was no hatred with His love, no venom, no spite, no selfishness. He loved His enemies and prayed for His murderers. It was not a fickle love, but a changeless, eternal love. "I have loved you with an everlasting love" (Jer. 31:3 ESV), God says. How marvelous that is!

It is just this kind of love He wants us to have. He said, "A new commandment I give to you, that you love one another: just as I have loved you" (John 13:34 ESV). That is tremendous, to command me to love my brothers and sisters even as Jesus loves me. But that is what He says, and to do that I must have a heart like Jesus.

I know if we examine love we find that it includes all the other graces; but we will look into the heart of Jesus for some of them.

Jesus had a humble heart. He said of Himself, "I am humble and gentle at heart" (Matt. 11:29 NLT). Paul told us that He "made himself nothing by taking the very nature of a servant" (Phil. 2:7 NIV).

He did humble Himself, for, though He is the Lord of life and glory, He stooped to be born of a lowly virgin in a manger, worked as an unknown carpenter for thirty years, and chose to live with the poor, ignorant, and vile instead of the rich, noble, and learned. While Jesus never seemed ill at ease or constrained in the presence of those who were mighty with this world's greatness or wise with its learning, His simple, humble heart found its mates among the lowly, hardworking, common people. He cleaved to them. He would not be lifted up. They wanted to do it for Him, but He slipped away for prayer among the mountains and then returned and preached such a straight sermon that nearly all His disciples left Him.

Just before His death, He took the menial place of a slave, washed His disciples' feet, and then said, "I have given you an example, that you also should do just as I have done to you" (John 13:15 ESV).

How that helped me in The Salvation Army training school! My second day there they sent me into a dark little cellar to blacken half a cartload of dirty boots for the other cadets. The Devil came at me and reminded me that a few years before I had graduated from a university, had attended a leading theological school, had been pastor of a metropolitan church, had just left evangelistic work in which I saw hundreds seeking the Savior, and that now I was only blacking boots for a lot of ignorant lads. But I reminded my old Enemy of my Lord's example, and the Devil left me. Jesus said, "Now that you know these things, you will be blessed if you do them" (John 13:17 NIV). I was doing them; the Devil knew it and left me alone, and I was happy. That little cellar was changed into one of heaven's anterooms, and my Lord visited me there.

"God opposes the proud but shows favor to the humble" (James 4:6 NIV). If you would have a heart like that of Jesus, it will be one filled with humility. It will be a heart that "is not puffed up," that "does not seek its own" (1 Cor. 13:4–5 NKJV). So as Peter said, "Be clothed with humility" (1 Pet. 5:5 KJV).

Jesus had a meek and gentle heart. Paul spoke of "the meekness and gentleness of Christ" (2 Cor. 10:1 KJV). Peter told us that "when he was reviled, he did not revile in return; when he suffered, he did not threaten" (1 Pet. 2:23 ESV). He did not strike back when He was injured. He did not try to justify Himself, but committed His cause to His heavenly Father.

That was the very perfection of meekness, that not only would He not strike back when He was lied about, but suffered the most cruel and shameful wrongs. "Out of the abundance of the heart the mouth speaks" (Matt. 12:34 NKJV), and because meekness filled His blessed heart He did not thunder back at His enemies.

It is just this kind of heart He wants us to have: "Do not resist an evildoer. But if anyone strikes you on the right cheek, turn the other also . . . and if anyone forces you to go one mile, go also the second mile" (Matt. 5:39, 41 NRSV).

I know a brother of African descent, over six feet tall with a full chest and brawny arms, who was recently put off a streetcar in the most indecent and brutal manner, where he had as much right to be as the conductor. Someone asked, "Why don't you fight him, George?"

"I couldn't fight him," replied George. "For God has taken all the fight out of me. When you put your knife in the fire and draw the temper out of it, it won't cut," he added, and he fairly shouted for joy.

"Blessed are the meek" (Matt. 5:5 KJV), for "he crowns the humble with victory" (Ps. 149:4 NLT).

NOTES

1. Homer A. Rodeheaver, "Give Me a Heart Like Thine," 1922, public domain.

2. Charles Wesley, "O for a Heart to Praise My God," 1742, public domain.

The Secret of Power **8**

If I were dying and had the privilege of delivering a last exhortation to all the Christians of the world, and that message had to be condensed into three words, I would say, "Wait on God!"

Wherever I go, I find people—from various church backgrounds—falling away from faith by the thousands, until my heart aches as I think of the great army of discouraged souls, of the way in which the Holy Spirit has been grieved, and of the way in which Jesus has been treated.

If these wayward ones were asked the cause of their present condition, ten thousand different reasons would be given. But, after all, there is only one, and that is this: they did not wait on God. If they had waited on Him when the fierce assault was made that overthrew their faith and robbed them of their courage and bankrupted their love, they would have renewed their strength and mounted over all obstacles as though on eagles' wings. They would have run through their enemies and not been weary. They would have walked in the midst of trouble and not fainted.

Waiting on God means more than a prayer of thirty seconds on getting up in the morning and going to bed at night. It may mean one prayer that gets hold of God and comes away with the blessing, or it may mean a dozen prayers that knock and persist and will not be put off until God arises and bares His arm on behalf of the pleading soul.

There is a drawing near to God—a knocking at heaven's doors, a pleading of the promises, a reasoning with Jesus, a forgetting of self, a turning from all earthly concerns, a holding on with determination to never let go—that puts all the wealth of heaven's wisdom and power and love at our disposal, little though we may be, so that we shout and triumph when all others tremble and fail and fly, and become more than conquerors in the very face of death and hell.

It is in the heat of just such seasons of waiting on God that every great soul gets the wisdom and strength that make it an astonishment to others. They, too, might be "great in the sight of the Lord" (Luke 1:15 KJV), if they would wait on God and be true instead of getting excited and running here and there for help when the testing times come.

The psalmist had been in great trouble, and this is what he said of his deliverance: "I waited patiently for the LORD to help me, and he turned to me and heard my cry. He lifted me out of the pit of despair, out of the mud and the mire. He set my feet on solid ground and steadied me as I walked along. He has given me a new song to sing, a hymn of praise to our God. Many will see what he has done and be amazed. They will put their trust in the LORD" (Ps. 40:1–3 NLT).

I went to a poor little corps (The Salvation Army church) where nearly everything had been going wrong. Many were cold and discouraged, but I found one sister with a wondrous glory in her face, and glad, sweet praises in her mouth. She told me how she had looked at others falling around her, had seen the carelessness of many, and had noted the decline of vital piety in the corps, until her heart ached and she felt disheartened and her feet almost slipped. But she went to God and got down low before Him. She prayed and waited until He drew near to her and showed her the awful precipice on which she herself was standing. He showed her that her one business was to follow Jesus, to walk before Him with a perfect heart, and to cleave to Him, though the whole corps lost faith. Then she renewed her covenant until an unutterable joy came to her heart and God put His fear in her soul and filled her with the glory of His presence.

She told me that the next day she fairly trembled to think of the awful danger she had been in and declared that that time of waiting on God in the silence of the night saved her, and now her heart was filled with the full assurance of hope for herself, and not only for herself, but also for the corps. Oh, for ten thousand more like her!

David said, "My soul, wait silently for God alone, for my expectation is from Him" (Ps. 62:5 NKJV). Again he declared: "I wait for the LORD, my whole being waits, and in his word I put my hope. I wait for the LORD more than watchmen wait for the morning" (Ps. 130:5–6 NIV). And David sent out this ringing exhortation and note of encouragement to you and me: "Wait patiently for the LORD. Be brave and courageous. Yes, wait patiently for the LORD" (Ps. 27:14 NLT).

The secret of all failures—and all true success—is hidden in the attitude of the soul in its private walk with God. We who courageously wait on God are bound to succeed. We cannot fail. To others we may appear for the present to fail, but in the end they will see what we knew all the time: that God was with us, making us successful, in spite of all appearances (see Gen. 39:2).

Jesus put the secret into these words: "When you pray, go into your room and shut the door and pray to your Father who is in secret. And your Father who sees in secret will reward you" (Matt. 6:6 ESV).

Know, then, that all failure has its beginning in the closet, in neglecting to wait on God until filled with wisdom, clothed with power, and all on fire with love.

The Leakage of Spiritual Power 9

James Caughey, a man of God and lover of souls, told in one of his books how he was invited out to tea one evening and, though there was nothing harmful in the talk of the hour, when he went into the revival meeting at night his soul was like a loosely strung bow. He couldn't shoot the King's arrows into the hearts of the King's enemies, for he had no power. It had been lost at the tea table.[1]

I knew an officer (The Salvation Army minister) once who let all his spiritual power leak out until he was as dry as an old bone when he got into the meeting. It was in this way. We had to ride three miles in a street car to get to the hall, and all the way there he was talking about things that had no bearing upon the coming meeting. Nothing wrong or trifling was said, but it was not to the point; it turned his mind from God and the souls he was so soon to face and plead with to be reconciled to God. The result was that instead of going before the people clothed with power, he went stripped of power. I remember the meeting well. His prayer was good, but there was no power in it. It was words, words, words! The Bible reading and talk were good. He said many true and excellent things, but there was no power in them. The soldiers (church members) looked indifferent, the others in attendance looked careless and sleepy, and altogether the meeting was a dull affair.

That officer had not faltered in his faith; he had a good experience. Nor was he unintelligent; on the contrary, he was one of the brightest, keenest officers I know. The trouble was that, instead of keeping quiet and communing with God in his own heart on that car, until his soul was ablaze with faith and hope and love and holy expectation, he had wasted his power in useless talk.

God says, "If you speak good words rather than worthless ones, you will be my spokesman" (Jer. 15:19 NLT). Think of it! That officer might have gone into that meeting filled with power. His mouth should have been to those people as the mouth of God, and his words would have been "living and powerful, and sharper than any two-edged sword, piercing even to the division of soul and spirit, and of joints and marrow," and proving to be "a discerner of the thoughts and intents of the heart" (Heb. 4:12 NKJV). But instead of that, he was like Samson after his locks were shorn by Delilah—as powerless as anyone else.

There are many ways of letting spiritual power leak away. I knew a soldier who came to The Salvation Army meeting hall very early every evening, and instead of getting his soul keyed up to a high pitch of faith and love, spent the time playing soft, dreamy music on his violin, and though faithfully, lovingly warned, continued that practice till he lost his faith.

I have also known people whose power leaked out through a joke. They believed in making things lively, so they told funny stories and played the clown. And things were lively, but it was not with divine life. It was the liveliness of mere animal spirits, and not of the Holy Spirit. I do not mean by this that someone who is filled with the power of the Spirit will never make others laugh. He or she will and may say tremendously funny things. But this person will not be doing it just to have a good time. It will come naturally, and it will be done in the fear of God and not in a spirit of lightness and jesting.

There is no substitute for the Holy Spirit. He is life. He is power. And if He is sought in earnest, faithful prayer, He will come, and when He comes the little meeting will be mighty in its results.

The Holy Spirit should be sought in earnest, secret prayer. Jesus said, "When you pray, go away by yourself, shut the door behind you, and pray to your Father in private. Then your Father, who sees everything, will reward you" (Matt. 6:6 NLT). He will do it.

I know of a man who, if possible, gets alone with God for an hour before every meeting, and when he speaks it is with the power and demonstration of the Spirit.

People who want power when it is most needed must walk with God. They must be friends of God. They must keep the way always open between their hearts and God. God will be the friend of such souls and will bless and honor them. God will tell them His secrets. He will show them how to appeal to the hearts of others. God will make dark things light, crooked places straight, and rough places smooth for such men and women. God will be on their side and help them.

Such a man or woman must keep a constant watch over the mouth and the heart. David prayed, "Set a watch, O LORD, before my mouth; keep the door of my lips" (Ps. 141:3 KJV). And Solomon said, "Guard your heart above all else, for it determines the course of your life" (Prov. 4:23 NLT). We must walk in unbroken communion with God. We must cultivate a spirit of joyful recollection by which we will be always conscious that we are in God's presence.

"Take delight in the LORD," said the psalmist, "and he will give you your heart's desires" (Ps. 37:4 NLT). Oh, how happy are they who find God to be their delight, who are never lonely, because they know God, talk with God, and delight in God. Happy are they who feel how lovable God is and give themselves up to loving, serving, and trusting God with all their hearts!

Brothers and sisters, "Do not stifle the Holy Spirit" (1 Thess. 5:19 NLT), and He will lead you thus to know and love God, and God will make you the instrument of His own power.

NOTE

1. This is most likely in reference to chapter 44 in James Caughey, *Showers of Blessing from Clouds of Mercy* (Boston: J. P. Magee, 1857), 325–327.

The Person God Uses 10

A while ago I was talking with a Christian merchant who expressed a great and important truth. He said, "People are crying to God to use them, but He cannot. They are not given up to Him. They are not humble and teachable and holy. There are plenty of people who come to me and want work in my store, but I cannot use them; they are not fit for my work. When I must have someone, I have to go and advertise, and sometimes spend days in trying to find a man who will fit into the place I want him for, and then I have to try him and prove him to know whether he will suit me or not."

The fact is, God is using everyone He can and using them to the full extent of their fitness for His service. So instead of praying so much to be used, people should search themselves to know whether they are usable.

God cannot use anybody and everybody who comes along any more than the merchant could. Only those who are "holy, useful to the Master and prepared to do any good work" (2 Tim. 2:21 NIV) can He bless with great usefulness.

God wants men and women, and He is hunting for them everywhere. But like the merchant, He has to pass by hundreds before He finds the right individuals. The Bible says, "For the eyes of the LORD run to and fro throughout the whole earth, to shew himself strong in the behalf of them whose heart is perfect toward him" (2 Chron. 16:9 KJV).

Oh, how God wants to use you! But before you ask Him again to do so, see to it that your heart is perfect toward Him. Then you may depend upon it that God will show Himself strong on your behalf.

When God searches for a man or woman to work in His vineyard, He does not ask, "Has he great natural abilities? Is she thoroughly educated? Is he a fine singer? Is she eloquent in prayer?"

Rather, He asks, "Is his heart perfect toward Me? Is she holy? Does he love much? Is she willing to walk by faith and not by sight? Does he love Me so much and has he such childlike confidence in My love for him that he can trust Me to use him when he doesn't see any sign that I am using him? Will she be weary and faint when I correct her and try to fit her for greater usefulness? Or will she, like Job, cry out, 'Though he slay me, yet will I trust in him' (Job 13:15 KJV)? Does he search My Word, and 'meditate on it day and night' in order to 'be sure to obey everything written in it' (Josh. 1:8 NLT)? Does he wait on Me for My counsel and seek in everything to be led by My Spirit? Or is he stubborn and self-willed, like the horse and the mule, which have to be held in with bit and bridle, so that I cannot 'guide him with mine eye' (Ps. 32:8 KJV)? Is she a people-pleaser and a time-server, or is she willing to wait for her reward, seeking solely for 'the honor that comes from the only God' (John 5:44 NKJV)? Does he 'preach the word' and is he 'ready in season and out of season' (2 Tim. 4:2 NASB)? Is she meek and lowly in heart and humble?"

When God finds someone like that, He will use him or her. God and that person will have such a friendly understanding with each other and such mutual sympathy and love and confidence that they will at once become partners (see 2 Cor. 6:1).

Paul was a man God used, and the more his persecutors whipped and stoned him and tried to rid the earth of him, the more God used him. At last they shut him up in prison, but Paul declared with unshaken faith, "I am suffering, bound with chains as a criminal. But the word of God is not bound!" (2 Tim. 2:9 ESV). And so he spoke God's Word, and neither devils nor mortals could shackle it, but it pierced right through the prison walls and flew across oceans and continents and down through the long centuries, bearing the glorious tidings of the blessed gospel, overthrowing thrones and kingdoms and powers of evil, and everywhere bringing light and comfort and salvation to dark, troubled, sinful hearts. Though more than eighteen hundred years have passed since they cut off Paul's head and thought they were done with him forever, yet his usefulness increases and his mighty words and works are today bearing such fruit to the good of humanity and the glory of God as passes the comprehension of an archangel.

Oh, how surprised Paul will be when he receives his final reward at the general judgment day and enters into possession of all the treasures he has laid up in heaven and the everlasting inheritance prepared for him!

Poor, troubled soul, cheer up! You think you are useless, but be of good courage! Trust God!

Paul saw dark days. He wrote to Timothy and said, "As you know, everyone from the province of Asia has deserted me" (2 Tim. 1:15 NLT). Study Paul's life in the Acts and the Epistles and see what conflicts and discouragements he had, and take courage!

Jesus said, "Anyone who believes in me may come and drink! For the Scriptures declare, 'Rivers of living water will flow from his heart.' (When he said 'living water,' he was speaking of the Spirit, who would be given to everyone believing in him)" (John 7:38–39 NLT).

See to it that you are a believer. See to it that you are "filled with the Holy Spirit" (Eph. 5:18 NLT), and Jesus will see to it that out of your life shall flow rivers of holy influence and power to bless the world. And you, too, will be surprised, at the reckoning day, to behold the vastness of your reward as compared with the littleness of your sacrifices and your work.

I was once asked, "Cannot one take too much care of one's own soul? I see all about me, everywhere, so much sorrow and suffering and injustice that I am perplexed at God's way of ruling the world, and it seems to me as though every Christian ought to be trying to help others instead of looking out for one's own soul."

This is a common perplexity. We see all around us sorrow and suffering which we cannot help, and our perplexity at the sight is the Lord's prompting for us to take the very uttermost care of our own souls, lest we stumble and fall through doubt and discouragement.

By the care of your soul I do not mean that you should coddle and pet and pity yourself, nor work yourself up into some pleasant feeling. I mean that you should pray and pray and pray and seek the presence and teaching of the Holy Spirit, until light and strength fill your soul such that you may have unquestioning faith in the wisdom and love of God, you may have unwearied patience in learning His will (see Heb. 6:12), and your love may be equal to the great need you see all about you.

Maybe you are troubled by the sight of unhelped wretchedness near you. No living soul can answer to your satisfaction the questions that will rise up within you nor counter the suggestions of Satan as you look on the world's misery. But the blessed Comforter will satisfy your heart and your head if you have the faith and patience to wait while He teaches you "all things" and leads you "into all truth" (John 16:13 KJV).

"They who wait for the LORD shall renew their strength" (Isa. 40:31 ESV). You cannot help people if you go to them robbed of your strength because of doubts, fears, and perplexities. So, wait on God till He strengthens your heart.

Do not become impatient. Do not try beforehand to find out what God will say or just how He will say it. He will surely teach you, but you must let Him do it in His own way, and then you will be able to help people with all the might and wisdom of Jehovah.

You must trust His love and abide His time, but you also must wait on Him and expect Him to teach you. If the king or queen of England is coming to Windsor Castle, the servants do not lie around listlessly nor hunt up a lot of work to do; everyone stands in his or her own place and waits with eager expectancy. This is what I mean by waiting upon God. You cannot do too much of this kind of taking care of your own soul, and do not let anyone drive you from it by ridicule or entreaty.

The woodsman would be very foolish who thought he had so much wood to cut that he could not take time to grind his ax. The servant who went to the city to buy things for her master would be useless if she was in such a hurry that she did not come to her master for orders and the needed money. How much worse are those who attempt to do God's work without God's direction and God's strength!

One morning, after a half-night of prayer which I led, and in which I had worked very hard, I got up early to ensure an hour with God and my Bible, and God blessed me till I wept. An officer (minister) who was with me was much moved and then confessed, "I do not often find God in prayer—I have not time." People who do not find God in prayer must hinder His cause instead of helping it.

Take time. Miss breakfast if necessary, but take time to wait on God, and when God has come and blessed you, then go to the miserable ones around you and pour upon them the wealth of joy, love, and peace God has given you. But do not go until you know you are going in His power.

I once heard William Booth say in a gathering of officers, "Take time to pray God's blessing down on your own soul every day. If you do not, you will lose God. God is leaving men every day. They once had power. They walked in the glory and strength of God but they ceased to wait on Him and earnestly seek His face, and He left them. I am a very busy man, but I take time to get alone with God every day and commune with Him."

Paul said, "Keep watch over yourselves and over all the flock, of which the Holy Spirit has made you overseers" (Acts 20:28 NRSV). And again, "Pay close attention to yourself and to your teaching; persevere in these things, for as you do this you will ensure salvation both for yourself and for those who hear you" (1 Tim. 4:16 NASB).

Paul did not mean to promote selfishness by telling us to first take heed to ourselves. But he did mean to teach that, unless we do take heed to ourselves and are full of faith, hope, and love in our own souls, we shall be unable to help others.

Gideon's Band   12

One hundred and twenty thousand Midianites had come up to fight against Israel, and thirty-two thousand Israelites rose up to fight for their wives, children, homes, liberty, and lives. But God saw that if one Israelite whipped nearly four Midianites, he would be so puffed up with pride and conceit that he would forget God, and say, "My own hand has saved me" (Judg. 7:2 ESV).

The Lord also knew that there were a lot of weak-kneed followers with cowardly hearts among them, who would like an excuse to run away. So He told Gideon to say, "Whoever is fearful and trembling, let him return home and hurry away" (Judg. 7:3 ESV). The sooner fearful folks leave us the better. "Then 22,000 of the people returned, and 10,000 remained" (Judg. 7:3 ESV). They were afraid to show the enemy their faces, but they were not ashamed to show them their backs.

But the Lord saw that if one Israelite whipped twelve Midianites he would be even more puffed up, so he made a further test.

He said to Gideon, "The people are still too many. Take them down to the water, and I will test them for you there" (Judg. 7:4 ESV). God often tries people at the table and the teapot.

So he brought the people down to the water. And the LORD said to Gideon, "Every one who laps the water with his tongue, as a dog laps, you shall set by himself. Likewise, every one who kneels down to drink." And the number of those who lapped, putting their hands to their mouths, was 300 men, but all the rest of the people knelt down to drink water. And the LORD said to Gideon, "With the 300 men who lapped I will save you and give the Midianites into your hand, and let all the others go every man to his home." (Judg. 7:5–7 ESV)

These three hundred men meant business. They were not only unafraid, but they were also not self-indulgent. They knew how to fight, but they knew something even more important—how to deny themselves. They knew how to deny themselves, not only when there was very little water, but when a river rolled at their feet. They were no doubt quite as thirsty as the others, but they did not throw down their arms and fall down on their faces to drink while in the presence of the enemy. They stood up, kept their eyes open, watched the enemy, and kept one hand on shield and bow, while with the other they brought water to their thirsty lips. The other fellows were not afraid to fight, but they would drink first, even if the enemy did steal a march on them while they were prostrate on the ground satisfying their thirst. Number one must be cared for, even if the army was crushed. They were self-indulgent and never dreamed of denying themselves for the common good, so God sent them home along with those who were afraid, and with the three hundred He routed the Midianites. That was one to four hundred. No chance of self-conceit there! They won the victory and became immortal, but God got the glory.

There are fearful people who cannot face a laugh or a sneer, much less a determined foe. If they cannot be led to lay hold of the strength and boldness of the Lord, the sooner they quit the field, the better. Let them go back to their spouses, children, and parents.

But there are many who are not afraid. They rather enjoy a fight. They would just as soon march in the streets, face a mob, and sing and pray and testify in the presence of enemies as they would stay at home—perhaps more so. But they are self-indulgent. If they like a thing they must have it, however much it may hurt them and make them unfit for the fight.

I am acquainted with some people who know that tea, cake, and candy injure them, but they like these things, and so they indulge themselves at the risk of grieving the Spirit of God and destroying their health, which is the capital God has given them to do His work with.

I know some people who ought to know that a big supper before a worship service or evangelistic meeting taxes the digestive organs, draws the blood from the head to the stomach, and makes one drowsy, dull, and heavy. Thus it unfits the soul to feel spiritual realities keenly and to stand between God and the people, pleading with God in mighty, believing, Elijah-like prayer, and prevailing with the people in clear testimony and burning exhortation. But they are hungry. They like such things, and so they tickle their palate with the things they like, punish their stomachs, spoil their meetings, disappoint the starving, hungry souls of the people, and grieve the Holy Spirit—all to gratify their appetites.

I know people who cannot watch with Jesus through a half-night of prayer without buns and coffee. Imagine Jacob in that desperate all-night of prayer wrestling with the angel for the blessing before meeting his injured brother Esau in the morning, stopping to have buns and coffee! If his soul had been no more desperate than that, he could have had his buns, but on his return to wrestle he would have found the angel gone. And the next morning, instead of learning that the angel who had disjointed his thigh (but left his blessing) had also melted Esau's hard heart, he would have found an angry brother, who would have been ready to carry out his threat of twenty years before and take his life. But Jacob was desperate. He wanted God's blessing so much that he forgot all about his body. In fact, he prayed so earnestly that his thigh was put out of joint, and he did not complain. He had gained the blessing.

When Jesus prayed, agonized, and sweated great drops of blood in the garden, His disciples slept, and He was grieved that they could not watch with Him one hour. And He must be grieved today that so many cannot, or will not, watch with Him and so deny their inmost self to win victory over the powers of hell and snatch souls from the bottomless pit.

We read of Daniel, that for three long weeks he ate no pleasant food, but gave himself to prayer during all the time he possibly could, so eager was he to know the will of God and get the blessing. And he got it. One day God sent an angel who said to him, "O man greatly beloved" (Dan. 10:19 KJV) and then told him all he wanted to know.

In Acts 14:23, we read that Paul and Barnabas prayed and fasted—not feasted—that the people might be blessed before they left the churches of Asia Minor. They were greatly interested in the souls they left behind them.

We know that Moses, Elijah, and Jesus fasted and prayed for forty days and, immediately after, mighty works were done.

And so, all mighty men and women of God have learned to deny themselves and keep their bodies under discipline, and God has set their souls on fire, helped them to win victory against all odds, and blessed the whole world.

We should not deny ourselves food and drink to the injury of our bodies. But one night of watching and fasting and praying can starve no one. And those who are willing to forget their bodies occasionally for a short time, in the interest of their own souls and the souls of others, will reap blessings which will amaze them and all who know them.

But this self-restraint must be constant. It will not do to fast all night and feast all the next day. The apostle Paul wrote of being "temperate in all things" (1 Cor. 9:25 KJV)—and he might have added, "at all times."

Again, Gideon's band did some night work, or early morning work. They got ahead of their enemies by getting up early (see Judg. 7:19).

People who indulge their bodies in food and drink also usually indulge them in sleep. They eat late at night and sleep heavily and lazily the next morning, and usually need a cup of strong coffee or tea to clear their heads. By getting up late, the work of the day crowds upon them and they have almost no time to praise the Lord, pray, and read the Bible. Then the day's cares press upon them and their hearts get full of things other than the joy of the Lord. Jesus must wait till they have done everything else before He can catch their ear, and so their day is spoiled.

Oh, that they knew the advantage, the luxury, the hilarious joy of early rising to fight the Midianites! It seems that Gideon, the captain, was up and about all night. He roused his people early, and they had the Midianites all whipped and scattered before dawn.

Four hundred devils cannot stand before the man or woman who makes it a rule of life to get up early to praise the Lord and plead for God's blessing on his or her own soul and on the world. They will flee away.

John Fletcher used to mourn if he knew of a laborer getting out to his daily toil before he himself was up praising God and fighting the Devil. He said, "What! Does that man's earthly master deserve more ready service than my heavenly Master?" Another old saint lamented greatly if he heard the birds singing before he got up to praise God.

We read that Jesus arose early and went out alone to pray. Joshua, we learn, got up early in the morning to set battle in array against Jericho and Ai.

John Wesley went to bed at ten o'clock sharp—unless he had an all-night prayer—and woke promptly at four. Six hours of sleep was all he wanted. And when he was eighty-two years old, he said he was a wonder to himself, for during the twelve years previous he had not been sick a day, nor felt weary, nor lost an hour's sleep, although he traveled thousands of miles each year, in winter and summer, on horseback and in carriages, as he preached hundreds of sermons, and did work that not one in a thousand could do. All of this he attributed to the blessing of God on his simple, plain way of living and to a clear conscience. He was a very wise and useful man, and he considered the matter of such grave importance that he wrote and published a sermon on "Redeeming the Time" from sleep.

A captain (experienced officer) in The Salvation Army wrote me the other day that he had begun to do his praying in the morning when his mind was fresh and before the cares of the day had begun to rush in on him.

It means more to belong to Gideon's band than most people ever dreamed of, but I have joined it, and my soul is on fire. It is a joy to live and belong to such a company.

The Chained Ambassador 13

My soul was stirred the other morning by Paul's appeal for the prayers of the church, in which he declared himself to be "an ambassador in chains" (Eph. 6:20 ESV).

You know what an ambassador is—a person who represents one government to another. The person of such a man or woman is considered sacred. Their words are powerful. The dignity and authority of their country and government stands behind them. Any injury or indignity to them is an injury and indignity to the country they represent.

Now Paul was an ambassador of heaven, representing the Lord Jesus Christ to the people of this world. But instead of being respected and honored, he was thrust into prison and chained between two ignorant, and probably brutal, Roman soldiers.

What stirred me was the quenchless zeal of the man and the work he did in the circumstances. Most Christians would have considered their work done or, at least, broken off till they were free again. But not so with Paul. From his prison and chains, he sent forth a few letters that have blessed the world and will bless it to the end of time. He also taught us that there is a ministry of prayer, as well as of more active work. We live in an age of restless work and rush and excitement, and we need to learn this lesson.

Paul was the most active of all the apostles—"in labours more abundant" (2 Cor. 11:23 KJV)—and it seemed as if he could hardly be spared from the oversight of the new Christians and the new churches he had so recently opened, which were in such desperate circumstances and surrounded by implacable enemies. But as he was set to be the chief exponent of the doctrines of the gospel of Christ, so he was set to be the chief exponent of its saving and sanctifying power under the most trying conditions.

It is difficult—if not impossible—to conceive of a trial to which Paul was not subjected, from being worshiped as a god to being whipped and stoned as the vilest slave. But he declared that none of these things moved him. He had learned in whatsoever state he was to be content (see Phil. 4:11), and he triumphantly wrote at the end of his life, "I have fought the good fight, I have finished the race, and I have remained faithful" (2 Tim. 4:7 NLT). He did not lose faith. He did not even murmur, but kept on his way, trusting in the love of Jesus, and, through faith in Him, coming off more than a conqueror.

Many have fairly well learned the lessons of activity Paul taught us, but it will be well for us all to learn the lessons his imprisonment teaches us. Doubly important is it for those who are sick or recovering to learn these lessons. We get impatient of waiting, are tempted to murmur and repine, and imagine that we can do nothing. But the fact is, God may possibly use us more widely in prayer and praise, if we will believe and rejoice and watch and pray in the Holy Spirit, than if He used us at the head of a battalion of soldiers. We should watch over in prayer those who are at work and for those in need of the salvation of God.

I write from experience. For eighteen months, I was laid aside with a broken head. God put His chain on me, and I had to learn the lessons of a passive ministry of prayer, praise, and patience, or lose faith altogether. It seemed as if I should never be able to work any more. But I did not lose faith. God helped me to nestle down into His will, and, like David, to behave and quiet myself, as a child weaned of his mother, until my soul was even as a weaned child (see Ps. 131:2). Yet my heart longed for the glory of God and the salvation of nations, and I prayed, watched reports of the salvation war, studied the needs of some parts of the world, and prayed on until I knew God heard and answered me. And my heart was made as glad as though I had been in the thick of the fight.

During that time I read of a great country, and my heart ached, burned, and longed for God to send salvation there. In secret and in family prayer, I poured out my heart to God, and I knew He heard and would yet do great things for that dark, sad country. Shortly after this, I learned of dreadful persecutions and the banishment of many simple, earnest Christians to this country, and while I was greatly grieved at their sufferings, yet I thanked God that He was taking this way to get the light of His glorious salvation into that loveless, needy land.

The fact is, sick and resting saints of God can move Him to bless the world if they have faith and will storm heaven with continuous prayers.

There are more ways to chain God's ambassadors than between Roman soldiers in Roman dungeons. If you are hopelessly sick, you are chained. If you are shut in by family cares and claims, you are chained. But remember Paul's chain, and take courage.

I sometimes hear those who have deserted their posts and lost their ministry lamenting their sad fate and declaring they can do nothing. Let them bow beneath God's judgment, kiss the hand that smites them, and no longer chafe under the chain that binds them, but cheerfully and patiently begin to exercise themselves in the ministry of prayer. If they are faithful, God may yet unloose their chain and let them out into the happier ministry of work. Esau sold his birthright for a mess of pottage and missed the mighty blessing he should have had—but he still received a blessing (see Gen. 27:38–40).

If we really long to see God's glory and souls saved rather than just to have a good time, why should we not be content to lie on a sickbed or stand by a loom and pray, as well as to stand on a platform and preach, if God will bless one as much as the other?

The man or woman on the platform can *see* much of the work and its fruit; the prayer warrior can only feel it. But the certainty of being in touch with God and being used by Him may be as great as or greater than that of one who sees with the eye. Many a revival has had its secret source in the closet of some poor washerwoman or blacksmith who prayed in the Holy Spirit but was chained to a life of desperate daily toil. The person on the platform gets glory on earth, but the neglected, unknown, or despised chained ambassador who prayed will share largely in the general triumph, and, it may be, will march by the King's side while the preacher comes on behind.

God sees not as we see. He looks at the heart, regards His children's cry, and marks for future glory and renown and boundless reward all those who cry and sigh for His honor and the salvation of souls.

God could have loosed Paul, but He did not choose to do so. But Paul did not grumble, sulk, fall into despair, or lose his joy and peace and faith and power. He prayed and rejoiced and believed. He thought about the poor little struggling churches and the weak souls he had left behind. He wrote to them, bore them on his heart, wept over them, and prayed for them night and day, and in so doing moved God to bless ten thousand times ten thousand folks whom he never saw and of whom he never even dreamed.

But let no one called of God imagine that this lesson of the chained ambassador is for those who are free to go. It is not. It is only for those who are in chains.

Faith: The Grace and the Gift 14

There is an important difference between the grace of faith and the gift of faith, and I fear that a failure to note this difference and to act accordingly has led many people into darkness, and possibly some have even been led to cast away all faith and to plunge into the black night of skepticism.

The grace of faith is that which is given to everyone to work with, and by which he or she can come to God. The gift of faith is that which is bestowed upon us by the Holy Spirit at the point where we have made free use of the grace of faith.

Those who are exercising the grace of faith say, "I believe God will bless me" and seek God wholeheartedly. They pray secretly and publicly. They search the Bible to know God's will. They talk with Christians about the way God deals with the soul. They take up every cross, and at last, when they have reached the limits of the grace of faith, God suddenly, by some word of Scripture, testimony, or inward reasoning, bestows upon them the gift of faith by which they are enabled to grasp the blessings they have been seeking. Then they no longer say, "I believe God will bless me," but they joyfully exclaim, "I believe God does bless me!" Then the Holy Spirit witnesses that it is done, and they shout for joy and declare, "I know God blesses me!" And they would not thank an angel to tell them that it is done, for they know it is done, and neither mortals nor devils can rob them of this assurance. Indeed, what I have here called the gift of faith might be called (and probably is by some) the assurance of faith. However, it is not the name but the fact that is important.

Now the danger lies in claiming the gift of faith before having fully exercised the grace of faith. For instance, a person is seeking the blessing of a clean heart. She says, "I believe there is such a blessing, and I believe God will give it to me." Now, believing this, she should at once seek it from God, and if she perseveres in seeking, she will surely find. But if someone comes up and gets her to claim it before she has by the grace of faith fought her way through the doubts and difficulties she has to meet, and before God has bestowed upon her the gift of faith, she will probably drift along for a few days or weeks and then fall back and probably conclude that there is no such blessing as a clean heart. She should be warned, instructed, exhorted, and encouraged to seek till she gets the assurance.

Or suppose someone is sick, and says, "There are some people who have been sick, and God has healed them, and I believe He will heal me." Having this faith, he should seek this healing from God. But if someone persuades him to claim healing before he has, by the grace of faith, worked his way through the difficulties that oppose him, and before God has bestowed upon him the gift of faith by which he receives the healing, he will probably crawl out of bed for a short time, find out he is not healed, get discouraged, and maybe call God a liar, or possibly declare that there is no God and cast away all confidence forever.

Or, again, suppose an officer or other minister has her heart set on seeing souls saved and reasons with herself that it is God's will to save souls. Then she declares, "I am going to believe for twenty souls to experience new life tonight"—but night comes and twenty souls are not saved. Then she wonders what was the matter. The Devil tempts her. She doubts and, probably, falls into skepticism.

What was the trouble? Why, she said she was going to believe before she had earnestly and intelligently wrestled and pleaded with God in prayer and listened for God's voice till God wrought in her the assurance that twenty souls should be saved. "God . . . rewards those who sincerely seek him" (Heb. 11:6 NLT).

"But," says someone, "should we not urge seekers to believe that God does the work?"

Yes, if you are certain that they have sought Him with all their hearts. If you feel sure they have exercised the grace of faith fully and yielded all, then urge them tenderly and earnestly to trust Jesus. But if you are not sure of this, beware of urging them to claim a blessing God has not given them. Only the Holy Spirit knows when a soul is ready to receive God's gift, and He will notify that person when he or she is to be blessed. So beware not to attempt to do the Holy Spirit's work yourself. If you help seekers too much, they may die on your hands. But if you walk closely with God in a spirit of humility and prayer, He will reveal to you the right word to say that will help them through.

Again, let no one suppose that the grace of faith will necessarily have to be exercised a long time before God gives the assurance. You may get the blessing almost at once, if you urge your claim with a perfect heart, fervently, without any doubt and without any impatience toward God. But, as the prophet said, "If [the vision] seems to tarry, wait for it; it will surely come, it will not delay" (Hab. 2:3 NRSV). "In just a little while, he who is coming will come and will not delay" (Heb. 10:37 NIV). If the blessing should tarry, do not think because it is delayed that it is therefore denied. But, like the woman who came to Jesus in Mark 7:26, press your claim in all meekness and lowliness of heart, with undaunted faith. He will in love soon say to you, "Your faith is great. Your request is granted" (Matt. 15:28 NLT).

Don't Argue 15

In seeking to lead a holy, blameless life, I have been helped at one point by the advice of two men and the example of two others.

Some years ago in Boston, I attended an all-night of prayer. It was a blessed time, and scores of people sought the blessing of a clean heart that night. The Scriptures were read, many prayers were offered, many songs were sung, and many testimonies and exhortations were given. But of all the many excellent things said that night, only one burned itself into my memory, never to be forgotten. Just before the meeting closed, Commissioner James Dowdle, speaking to those who had been to the penitent form, said, "Remember, if you want to retain a clean heart, don't argue!" There were twenty years of practical holiness behind that advice, and it fell on my ears like the voice of God.

In writing to young Timothy, the aged apostle Paul poured out his heart to one he loved as a son of the gospel. He sought to fully instruct him in the truth, so that on the one hand Timothy might escape all the snares of the Devil, walk in holy triumph and fellowship with God, and thus save himself, and on the other hand be "thoroughly equipped" to instruct and train others (2 Tim. 3:17 NIV). Among other earnest words, these have deeply impressed me: "Remind everyone about these things, and command them in God's presence to stop fighting over words. Such arguments are useless, and they can ruin those who hear them" (2 Tim. 2:14 NLT).

I take it that Paul meant by this, that instead of arguing with people and so losing time, and maybe temper, we are to go right for their hearts and do our best to win them for Christ and get them saved and sanctified.

He continued: "Again I say, don't get involved in foolish, ignorant arguments that only start fights. A servant of the Lord must not quarrel but must be kind to everyone, be able to teach, and be patient with difficult people. Gently instruct those who oppose the truth. Perhaps God will change those people's hearts, and they will learn the truth" (2 Tim. 2:23–25 NLT).

Clearly the apostle thought this advice was important, for he repeated it in writing to Titus: "Avoid foolish controversies and genealogies and arguments and quarrels about the law, because these are unprofitable and useless" (Titus 3:9 NIV).

I am certain that Paul was right in this. It takes fire to kindle fire, and it takes love to kindle love. Cold logic will not make anyone love Jesus, and it is only the one who loves who "is born of God" (1 John 4:7 KJV).

We who have had the gospel taught to us in such simplicity and purity can scarcely realize the awful darkness through which some have had to struggle, even in so-called Christian countries, to find the true light.

Years ago, among the luxurious and licentious nobility of France, the Marquis de Renty attained a purity of faith, simplicity of life and character, and cloudless communion with God that greatly adorned the gospel and proved a blessing, not only to the people of his own community and age, but also to many people of succeeding generations. His social position, wealth, and business ability led to him being associated with others in various enterprises of a secular and religious character, in all of which his faith and godly sincerity shone with remarkable luster.

In reading the story of his life a few years ago, I was struck by his great humility, his sympathy for the poor and uneducated (and his zealous, self-denying efforts to instruct and save them), his diligence and fervor in prayer and praise, and his constant hungering and thirsting after all the fullness of God. But what impressed me as much as, or more than, all the rest was the way he avoided all argument of any nature, for fear he might grieve the Holy Spirit and quench the light in his soul. Whenever matters of a business or religious nature were discussed, he carefully thought the subject over and then clearly, fully, and quietly expressed his views and the reasons upon which he based them. Then, however heated the discussion might become, he declined to be drawn into any further debate. His quiet, peaceful manner, added to his clear statements, gave great force to his counsels. But whether his views were accepted or rejected, he always went to his opponents afterward and told them that, in expressing sentiments contrary to their own, he acted with no intention of opposing them personally, but simply that of declaring what seemed to him to be the truth.

In this he seems to me to have been closely patterned after "the meekness and gentleness of Christ" (2 Cor. 10:1 KJV), and his example has encouraged me to follow a like course, and so "keep the unity of the Spirit in the bond of peace" (Eph. 4:3 KJV), when otherwise I should have been led into wranglings and disputes which would have clouded my soul and destroyed my peace, even if the Holy Spirit were not utterly driven from my heart.

The enemies of Jesus were constantly trying to entangle Him in His words and involve Him in arguments, but He always turned the subject in such a way as to confound His foes and take every argument out of their mouths.

They came to Him one day and asked whether it was lawful to pay tribute to Caesar or not. Without any discussion, He asked for a coin. He then asked whose image was on the coin.

"Caesar's," they replied.

"Well, then," He said, "give to Caesar what belongs to Caesar, and give to God what belongs to God" (Matt. 22:21 NLT).

On another occasion, they brought to Him a woman who had been caught in the act of adultery. His loving heart was touched with compassion for her, but instead of arguing with her captors as to whether she should be stoned or not, He simply said, "Let the one who has never sinned throw the first stone!" (John 8:7 NLT). And the whole crowd of hypocrites was so convicted and baffled by His simplicity, that they sneaked out one by one until the woman was left alone with her Savior.

And so, all through the Gospels, I fail to find Jesus engaged in argument, and His example is of infinite importance to us.

It is natural to the "carnal mind" to resent opposition. But we are to be "spiritually minded" (Rom. 8:6 KJV). By nature we are proud of our persons and protective of our opinions, and we are ready to stoutly resist those who oppose either us or our principles. Our object at once is to subdue others, whether by force of argument or force of arms. We are impatient of contradiction and are hasty in judging others' motives and condemning all who do not agree with us. And then we are apt to call our haste and impatience "zeal for the truth," when, in fact, it is often a hotheaded, unkind, and unreasoning zeal for our own way of thinking. I am strongly inclined to believe that this is one of the last fruits of the carnal mind which grace ever subdues.

But let us who have become "partakers of the divine nature" (2 Pet. 1:4 KJV) see to it that this root of the carnal nature is utterly destroyed. When others oppose us, let us not argue, revile, or condemn, but lovingly instruct them—not with an air of superior wisdom and holiness, but with meekness, solemnly remembering that "the LORD's servant must not be quarrelsome but kindly to everyone, an apt teacher, patient, correcting opponents with gentleness" (2 Tim. 2:24–25 NRSV).

I find that often, after having plainly, fully, and calmly stated my views to one who is opposing the truth as I see it, I am strongly tempted to strive for the last word. But I also find that God blesses me most when I then commit the matter into His hands, and by so doing I most often win my adversary. I believe this is the way of faith and the way of meekness. While it may seemingly leave us defeated, we generally win our foe in the end. And if we have true meekness, we shall rejoice more over having won him or her to "a knowledge of the truth" (2 Tim. 2:25 NIV) than in having won an argument.

Letting the Truth Slip 16

The truth that saves the soul is not picked up as we would pick up the pebbles along the beach. Rather, it is obtained as gold and silver, after diligent searching and much digging. Solomon said, "If you call out for insight and raise your voice for understanding, if you seek it like silver and search for it as for hidden treasures, then you will understand the fear of the LORD and find the knowledge of God" (Prov. 2:3–5 ESV). Those who seek to obtain the truth will have to use their wits. They will need much prayer, self-examination, and self-denial. They must listen diligently in their own soul for God's voice. They must watch lest they fall into sin and forgetfulness, and must meditate in the truth of God day and night.

Men and women who are full of the truth—who are walking embodiments of the truth—have not become so without effort. They have dug for truth. They have loved it. They have longed for it more than for their necessary food. They have sacrificed all for it. When they have fallen, they have risen again, and when defeated they have not yielded to discouragement, but with more care and watchfulness and greater earnestness, they have renewed their efforts to attain the truth. They have not counted their lives dear unto themselves so they might know the truth. Wealth, ease, fame, reputation, pleasure, and everything the world holds has been counted as dung and dross in their pursuit of truth. And just at that point where truth took precedence over all creation, they found it—the truth that saves the soul, satisfies the heart, answers the questions of life, and brings fellowship with God and joy unutterable and perfect peace.

Just as it costs effort to find the truth, so it requires watching to keep it. "Riches have wings"[1] and, if unguarded, fly away. So with truth. It will slip away if not earnestly heeded. "Buy the truth and do not sell it" (Prov. 23:23 NIV). It usually slips away little by little. It is lost as leaking water is lost—not all at once, but by degrees.

Here is a man who was once full of the truth. He loved his enemies and prayed for them. But, little by little, he neglected that truth that we should love our enemies, and it slipped away, and instead of love and prayer for his enemies has come bitterness and sharpness.

Another once poured out his money upon the poor and for the spread of the gospel. He was not afraid to trust God to supply all his wants. He was so full of truth that all fear was gone, and he was certain that if he sought "first the kingdom of God, and his righteousness," all other things would be added to him (Matt. 6:33 KJV). He did not fear that God would forget him and forsake him and leave his children to beg for bread. He served God gladly and with all his heart.

He was satisfied with a crust and was as happy and careless as the sparrow that tucks its tiny head under its little wing and goes to sleep, not knowing from where its breakfast is to come, but trusts to the great God who opens His hand and satisfies the desire of every living thing and gives them their food as they need it (see Ps. 145:15–16). But, little by little, the Devil's prudence got into his heart, and he let the truth of God's faithfulness and fatherly, provident care slip, and now he is stingy, grasping, and anxious about tomorrow and altogether unlike his liberal, loving Lord.

Here is another who was once praying all the time. She loved to pray. Prayer was the very breath of her life. But, little by little, she lost her grip on the truth that we "should always pray and never give up" (Luke 18:1 NLT), and now prayer is a cold, dead form with her.

Another once seized every opportunity for corporate worship. But he began to neglect the truth that we should not "stop meeting together with other believers, which some people have gotten into the habit of doing" (Heb. 10:25 CEB), and now he prefers going to the park, lake, or gym to attending public worship services.

Another once sprang to his feet the moment an opportunity to testify was given, and whenever he met someone on the street he would speak of the good things of God. But, little by little, he gave way to "obscenity, foolish talk or coarse joking, which are out of place" (Eph. 5:4 NIV), and neglected the truth "that everyone will have to give account on the day of judgment for every empty word they have spoken" (Matt. 12:36 NIV). He no longer remembers that the Bible says, "Death and life are in the power of the tongue" (Prov. 18:21 KJV) and that we must always "let [our] conversation be gracious and attractive" (Col. 4:6 NLT). As a result, he can now talk glibly on every subject but that of personal faith and holiness. The old, thoughtful, fiery testimony that stirred the hearts of others, warned scoffers, encouraged fainting, timid hearts, and brought cheer and strength to his brothers and sisters has given place to a few set phrases which have lost their meaning to his own heart and have about the same effect on others that big icicles would have on a fire, and which are altogether as fruitless as broken shells in last year's bird's nest.

Another once believed with all her heart that "women who profess godliness" should "adorn themselves in respectable apparel, with modesty and self-control, not with braided hair and gold or pearls or costly attire, but with . . . good works" (1 Tim. 2:9–10 ESV). But, little by little, she let the truth of God slip. She listened to the Tempter's smooth whisperings, and she fell as surely as Eve fell when she listened to the Devil and ate the forbidden fruit. Now, instead of neat, respectable apparel, she is decked out in gaudy and "costly attire," but she has lost "the beauty that comes from within, the unfading beauty of a gentle and quiet spirit, which is so precious to God" (1 Pet. 3:4 NLT).

But what shall these people do?

Let them remember the heights from which they have fallen, repent, and do their first works over again (see Rev. 2:5). Let them dig for truth again as miners dig for gold, and search for it as for hidden treasures, and they will find it again, for God "rewards those who sincerely seek him" (Heb. 11:6 NLT).

This may be hard work; it is hard to dig for gold. It may be slow work; so it is to search for hidden treasure. But it is sure work: "Keep on seeking, and you will find" (Luke 11:9 NLT). And it is necessary work. Your soul's eternal destiny depends upon it.

What shall those who have the truth do to prevent its slipping? First, heed the word of David to his son Solomon: "Observe and seek out all the commandments of the LORD your God" (1 Chron. 28:8 ESV). Second, do what God commanded Joshua: "Meditate on it day and night." For what? So you will be sure to obey some of the things written in it? No! "Everything written in it" (Josh. 1:8 NLT).

A young rabbi asked his old uncle if he might not study Greek philosophy. The old rabbi quoted the text, "This Book of the Law shall not depart from your mouth, but you shall meditate on it day and night" (Josh. 1:8 ESV), and then replied, "Find an hour that is neither day nor night; in that hour you may study Greek philosophy."

The blessed person of David's psalm is not only one who "who does not walk in step with the wicked or stand in the way that sinners take or sit in the company of mockers, but"—notice—"whose delight is in the law of the LORD, and who meditates on his law day and night" (Ps. 1:1–2 NIV).

If you want to hold the truth fast and not let it slip, you must read and reread the Bible. You must constantly refresh your mind with its truths, just as the diligent student constantly refreshes his mind by reviewing his textbooks and as the lawyer who wishes to succeed constantly studies his law books or the doctor her medical works.

John Wesley, in his old age, after having read and reread the Bible all his life, said of himself, "I am *homo unius libri*"—a man of one book.

The truth will surely slip if you do not refresh your mind by constantly reading and meditating on the Bible. The Bible is God's recipe book for making holy people. You must follow the recipe exactly if you want to be a holy, Christlike person. The Bible is God's guidebook to show men and women the way to heaven. You must pay strict attention to its directions and follow them accurately if you are ever to get there. The Bible is God's doctor's book to show people how to get rid of soul-sickness. You must diligently consider its diagnosis of soul-diseases and its methods of cure if you want soul-health.

Jesus said, "People won't live only by bread, but by every word spoken by God" (Matt. 4:4 CEB). And again He said, "The very words I have spoken to you are spirit and life" (John 6:63 NLT).

Third, "Do not quench the Spirit" (1 Thess. 5:19 NIV). Jesus calls the Holy Spirit "the Spirit of truth" (John 14:17; 15:26; 16:13 NIV). Therefore, if you do not wish the truth to slip, welcome the Spirit of truth into your heart and ask Him to abide with you. Cherish Him in your soul. Delight yourself in Him. Live in Him. Yield yourself to Him. Trust Him. Commune with Him. Consider Him your friend, your guide, your teacher, your comforter. Do not look upon Him as some school children look upon their teacher—as an enemy, as one to be outwitted, as one who is constantly watching for a chance to punish and reprove and discipline. Of course, the Holy Spirit will do this when necessary, but such a necessity grieves Him. His delight is to comfort and cheer the children of God. He is love! "Do not grieve the Holy Spirit of God, by whom you were sealed for the day of redemption" (Eph. 4:30 ESV).

NOTE

1. Francis Bacon, *Essays, Civil and Moral*, The Harvard Classics, vol. 3, part 1 (New York: P. F. Collier & Son, 1909–1914), n.p.

If You Have Lost the Blessing 17

When a person falls into sin, the difficulty in the way of restoration is in him- or herself, not in the Lord. It is difficult for us to trust one whom we have wronged, and the difficulty is doubled when that one has been a tender, loving friend. See the case of Joseph's brothers. They grievously wronged him by selling him into Egypt, and at last, when they discovered that he was alive and they were in his power, they were filled with fear.

But Joseph assured them of his goodwill and finally won their confidence by his kindness. This confidence was apparently perfect until the death of their father, Jacob, and then all their old fears revived.

Now that their father was dead, Joseph's brothers became fearful. "Now Joseph will show his anger and pay us back for all the wrong we did to him," they said.

So they sent this message to Joseph: "Before your father died, he instructed us to say to you: 'Please forgive your brothers for the great wrong they did to you—for their sin in treating you so cruelly.' So we, the servants of the God of your father, beg you to forgive our sin." When Joseph received the message, he broke down and wept. . . .

But Joseph replied, "Don't be afraid of me. Am I God, that I can punish you? . . . No, don't be afraid. I will continue to take care of you and your children." So he reassured them by speaking kindly to them. (Gen. 50:15–17, 19, 21 NLT)

If you have fallen into sin, see your situation in this simple story. By your sin you have done violence to your own sense of justice, and now it is next to impossible for you to trust your grievously wronged brother, Jesus. And yet His tender heart is close to breaking over your distrust: "Joseph wept when they spoke to him" (Gen. 50:17 ESV). If you have not committed the unpardonable sin—and you have not, if you have any desire whatsoever to be the Lord's—your first step is to renew your consecration to the Lord, confessing your sins. Then your second and only step is to cry out with Job, "Though he slay me, yet will I trust in him" (Job 13:15 KJV), and this ground you must steadfastly hold, till the witness comes of your acceptance.

Many people fail at this point by constantly looking for the same emotions and joy they had when they were first saved, and they refuse to believe because they do not have that same old experience. Do you remember that the children of Israel went into captivity several times after they had entered Canaan, but never did God divide Jordan for them again? God never took them in again in the same manner as at first. God says, "I will lead the blind in a way that they do not know, in paths that they have not known I will guide them" (Isa. 42:16 ESV). But if you are seeking the old experience, you are refusing to acknowledge that you are blind and are insisting upon going in the paths you have known. In other words, you want to walk by sight and not by faith. You must yield yourself to the Holy Spirit, and He will surely lead you into the Promised Land. Seek simply to be right with God. Do whatever He tells you to do. Trust Him, love Him, and He will come to you, for He (Jesus) "became for us . . . sanctification" (1 Cor. 1:30 NKJV). It is not a blessing you want, but the Blesser, whom you have shut out by your unbelief.

A recently sanctified man at the School of Theology in Boston said, "I have been here studying theology for three years, but now I have the *Theos* [God] in me." Be satisfied with Him by whatever way He may come, whether as King of Kings and Lord of Lords or as a humble, simple, peasant carpenter. Be satisfied with Him, and He will more and more fully reveal Himself to your childlike faith.

Do not be frightened by roaring lions; they are chained. Steadfastly refuse to wonder about the future, but trustfully rest in Him for the present moment. "Don't worry about tomorrow, for tomorrow will bring its own worries. Today's trouble is enough for today" (Matt. 6:34 NLT).

Satan wants to create great concern in your mind about your ability to persevere. Especially if you lost your experience through disobedience, Satan will flaunt that fact in your face. Remember, "My grace is sufficient for thee" (2 Cor. 12:9 KJV). Be sure not to worry about tomorrow.

I heard a friend pray, "Father, you know what intolerable anguish I have suffered by looking ahead and wondering if I could do so-and-so at such-and-such a time and place." Of course he would suffer. The simple remedy was not to look into the future but to "hold up the shield of faith to stop the fiery arrows of the devil" (Eph. 6:16 NLT). He was suffering from fiery arrows. Be sure of this: It is not Jesus who is torturing you with thoughts of the future, for He has commanded you, "Don't worry about tomorrow" (Matt. 6:34 NLT). "Resist the devil, and he will flee from you" (James 4:7 NLT). But when you come up to the point of obedience, be true, even if it takes your life. "If you remain faithful even when facing death, I will give you the crown of life" (Rev. 2:10 NLT). Be among those who win heaven's commendation: "They did not love their lives so much that they were afraid to die" (Rev. 12:11 NLT).

One woman who had lost the experience said, "I gave myself back to Jesus and trusted for some time without any feeling. A young lady came to the house, and I felt I ought to speak to her about her soul. It seemed very hard, but I told the Lord I would be true. I spoke to her. Tears filled her eyes, and joy filled my heart. The Blesser had come, and now she is sweetly trusting in Jesus." Give yourself back to God, and let your very life enter into the consecration.

A woman who had wandered for ten years, but had just been reclaimed and filled with the Holy Spirit, said the other night, "Put your all on the altar, and leave it there; do not take it back, and God's fire will surely come and consume the offering."

Do it. Do it! God will surely come if you can wait; and you can wait, if you mean business for eternity. "That is why the LORD says, 'Turn to me now, while there is time. Give me your hearts. Come with fasting, weeping, and mourning. Don't tear your clothing in your grief, but tear your hearts instead.' Return to the LORD your God, for he is merciful and compassionate, slow to get angry and filled with unfailing love. He is eager to relent and not punish" (Joel 2:12–13 NLT).

Soul-Winners and
Their Prayers
18

All great soul-winners have been people of much and mighty prayer, and all great revivals have been preceded and carried out by persevering, prevailing knee-work in the closet. Before Jesus began His ministry, when great multitudes followed Him, He spent forty days and nights in secret prayer and fasting (see Matt. 4:1–11).

Paul prayed without ceasing. Day and night his prayers and pleadings and intercessions went up to God (see Acts 16:25; Phil. 1:3–11; Col. 1:3, 9–11). The Pentecostal baptism of the Spirit and the three thousand who experienced new life in one day were preceded by ten days of prayer and praise and heart-searching and Scripture-searching (see Acts 2:4–6). And they continued in prayer until, on another day, five thousand were added to the church (see Acts 4:4), and "many of the Jewish priests were converted, too" (Acts 6:7 NLT).

Luther used to pray three hours a day, and he broke the spell of ages and set captive nations free. John Knox used to spend nights in prayer, crying to God, "Give me Scotland, or I die!" And God gave him Scotland. Richard Baxter stained the walls of his study with praying breath and sent a tide of salvation through all the land.

Over and over again, John Wesley in his journals—which, for lively interest, are next to the Acts of the Apostles—tells of half and whole nights of prayer in which God drew near and blessed people beyond expectation, and then he and his helpers were empowered to rescue England from paganism and send a revival of pure, aggressive religion throughout the whole earth.

David Brainerd used to lie on the frozen ground at night, wrapped in a bear's skin and spitting blood, and cry to God to save the native tribes of North America. And God heard him, and redeemed and sanctified men and women by the hundreds.

The night before Jonathan Edwards preached the wonderful sermon that started the revival which convulsed New England, he and some others spent the night in prayer.

A young man named David Livingstone, in Scotland, was appointed to preach at one of the great assemblies. Feeling his utter weakness, he spent the night in prayer, and the next day preached a sermon, and five hundred people entered into the kingdom of God. Oh, my Lord, raise up some praying people!

Charles Finney used to pray until whole communities were brought under the influence of the Spirit of God and no one could resist the mighty influence. At one time, he was so prostrated by his labors that his friends sent him on a voyage of rest to the Mediterranean Sea. But he was so intent upon the salvation of others that he could not rest, and on his return he got into an agony of soul for the evangelization of the world. At last, the earnestness and agony of his soul became so great that he prayed all day, till in the evening he got a restful assurance that God would carry on the work. On reaching New York, he delivered his "Revival Lectures," which were published at home and abroad and resulted in revivals all over the world. Then his writings fell into the hands of Catherine Booth and mightily influenced her, so that The Salvation Army is in part God's answer to that man's agonizing, pleading, prevailing prayer that God would glorify His own name and save the world.

A young American evangelist seems to unleash a "revival tornado" everywhere he goes, bringing hundreds of people to faith in Christ Jesus. I wondered what the secret of his power might be until a lady at whose house he stopped said he prayed all the time—so much so, she could hardly get him to his meals from his mighty wrestlings with God.

Before joining The Salvation Army, I was one day talking with Dr. Charles Cullis of Boston, that man of simple, wonder-working faith. He was showing me some photographs, and among them was one of Bramwell Booth, our Chief of the Staff (territorial leader), who later became the second General (worldwide leader) of The Salvation Army.

"There," said the doctor, "that man leads the mightiest holiness meetings in all England."

He then told me about those famous Whitechapel meetings. When I went to England, I determined, if possible, to find out the secret of them.

"For one thing," said an officer, "Mr. Bramwell used to conduct young men's meetings at headquarters at that time, and he used to ask each saved young fellow to spend five minutes alone with God every day, wherever they could get it, praying for those Friday night meetings. One, who is a brigadier[1] now and was then employed in a large warehouse, had to squeeze himself into a great wicker packing case to get a chance to pray for five minutes."

God has not changed. He waits to do the will of praying men and women.

Mr. Finney tells of a church in which there was a continuous revival for thirteen years. At last the revival stopped, and everybody feared and questioned why, till one day a tearful man arose and told how for thirteen years he had prayed every Saturday night till after midnight for God to glorify himself and save the people. But two weeks before, he had stopped this praying, and then the revival had stopped. If God will answer prayer like that, what a tremendous responsibility rests on us all to pray!

Oh, for a holy soldier in every corps and a believing member in every church, who would spend half of every Saturday night in prayer! Here is work for those who are convalescing and for people who cannot go into ministry because of insurmountable difficulties. You can do some needed knee-work.

But let no one imagine that prayer is easy work. It is difficult and amounts sometimes to an agony, but it will turn into an agony of joy in union and fellowship with Jesus.

The other day a Salvation Army captain, who prays an hour or more each morning and half an hour before his evening meeting, and who is very successful in getting souls saved, was lamenting to me that he often has to force himself to secret prayer. But all men and women of much prayer have suffered the same. The Reverend William Bramwell, who used to see hundreds of people saved and sanctified everywhere he went, prayed six hours a day, and yet he said he always went to secret prayer reluctantly. He had to pull himself up to it. And after he began to pray, he would often have dry seasons. But he persevered in faith, and the heavens would open, and he would wrestle with God until the victory came. Then when he preached, the clouds would break and rain down blessings on the people.

One man asked another the reason why Reverend Bramwell was able to say such new and wonderful things that brought blessings to so many people. "Because," said the other, "he lives so near the Throne that God tells him His secrets, and then he tells them to us."

The Reverend John Smith—whose life, William Booth once told me, had been a marvelous inspiration to him—always spent much time in prayer. He always found it hard to begin and then got so blessed that it was hard to stop. Everywhere he went, mighty revival waves also went with him.

This reluctance to secret prayer may arise from one or more of several causes. First, from wicked spirits. I imagine the Devil does not care much when he sees the majority of cold-hearted people on their knees in public, for he knows they do it simply because it is proper and fashionable. But he hates to see anyone on his or her knees in secret, for that one means business and, persevering in faith, is bound to move God and all heaven. So the devils oppose that person's efforts. Second, from the sluggishness of the body and mind, caused by sickness, loss of sleep, too much sleep, or overeating, which unduly taxes the digestive organs, clogs the blood, and dulls all the higher and nobler powers of the soul. Third, from a failure to respond quickly when we feel led by the Spirit to go to secret prayer. If, when we feel we should pray, we hesitate longer than is necessary and continue reading or talking when we could just as well be praying, the spirit of prayer will be quenched.

We should cultivate gladness at the thought of getting alone with Jesus in secret communion and prayer, as much as lovers expect pleasure and joy in each other's company. We should promptly respond to the inward call to prayer. "Resist the devil, and he will flee from you" (James 4:7 KJV). We must discipline our bodies and our wills, lest we become disqualified (see 1 Cor. 9:27). Jesus made it clear that we "should always pray and never give up" (Luke 18:1 NLT), and Paul enjoined us to "pray without ceasing" (1 Thess. 5:17 KJV).

One daredevil, praying, believing man or woman can get the victory for a whole city or nation sometimes. Elijah did on Mount Carmel. Moses did for backsliding Israel. Daniel did in Babylon. But if a number of people can be led to pray in this way, the victory will be all the more sweeping. Let no one imagine, in a wicked heart of unbelief, that God is grudging and unwilling to answer prayer. He is more willing to answer those whose hearts are right with Him than parents are to give bread to their children. When Abraham prayed for Sodom, God answered till Abraham stopped asking (see Gen. 18:22–33). And is He not often angry with us because we ask so timidly and for such small blessings, just as the prophet Elisha was angry with the king who struck the ground but three times when he should have done so five or six times (see 2 Kings 13:18–19)?

Let us come boldly to the throne of grace and ask largely, that our joy may be full (see Heb. 4:16)!

NOTE

1. Brigadier is a former rank between major and lieutenant-colonel of a commissioned (ordained) Salvation Army officer. It was usually given after thirty years of service.

Present-Day Witnesses to the Resurrection

19

I once knelt in prayer with a young woman who wanted to be holy. I asked if she would give up everything for Jesus. She answered that she would. I then thought I would put a hard test to her and asked if she would be willing to go to Africa as a missionary. She said, "Yes." Then we prayed, and while we were praying, she burst into tears and cried out, "O Jesus!"

She had never seen Jesus. She had never heard His voice, and before this hour she had no more idea of such a revelation of Jesus to her soul than someone who was born blind has of a rainbow. But she knew Him! She had no more need that someone should tell her this was Jesus than you have need of the light of a tallow candle to see the sun come up. The sun brings its own light, and so does Jesus.

She knew Him; she loved Him; she rejoiced in Him with "joy unspeakable and full of glory" (1 Pet. 1:8 KJV). And from that hour she testified of Him and followed Him—even to Africa—till one day He said to her, "Well done, good and faithful servant . . . enter thou into the joy of thy lord" (Matt. 25:23 KJV), and then she went to heaven, to behold with open vision His unveiled glory.

That young woman was a witness for Jesus—a witness that He is not dead but living, and as such was a witness to His resurrection. Such witnesses are needed in every age. They are needed today as much as in the days of the apostles. People's hearts are just as wicked, their pride just as stubborn, their selfishness just as universal, and their unbelief just as obstinate as at any time in the world's history, and it takes just as powerful evidence to subdue their hearts and beget living faith in them as it ever did.

There are two kinds of evidence, each of which seems to be necessary to get people to accept the truth and come to faith in Jesus Christ. They are: the evidence we get from history and the evidence we get from living men and women who speak of their experience.

In the Bible and in the writings of early Christians, we have the historical evidences of God's plans for us and His dealings with us, of the life and death and resurrection of the Lord Jesus, and of the coming of the Holy Spirit. But these records alone do not seem sufficient to destroy people's unbelief and bring them into humble, glad submission to God, and into childlike faith in His dear love. They may produce historical faith. That is, people may believe what these writings say about God, humankind, sin, life, death, judgment, heaven and hell, just as they believe what history says about Julius Caesar, Napoleon Bonaparte, or George Washington. And this faith may lead them to be very religious, build temples, deny themselves, and go through many forms of worship. It may prompt them to forsake gross outward sin and live lives of decorum and morality, and yet leave them dead to God. It does not lead them into that living union with the Lord Jesus which slays inward and outward sin, takes away the fear of death, and fills the heart with joyful hope of immortality.

The faith that saves is the faith that brings the life and power of God into the soul—a faith that makes the proud heart humble, the impatient heart patient, the stingy heart generous, the lustful heart clean and chaste, the liar truthful, and the thief honest. It transforms a flippant and foolish person into someone who is thoughtful and prudent. It changes a fighting, quarrelsome spirit into someone who is meek and gentle. It is a faith that purifies the heart, sets the Lord always before the eyes, and fills the soul with humble, holy, patient love toward God and others.

To beget this faith, what is needed is not only the Bible with its historical evidences, but also a living witness, one who has "tasted the good word of God, and the powers of the world to come" (Heb. 6:5 KJV), who knows that Jesus is not dead, but alive, and can witness to the resurrection, because he or she knows the Lord, who is "the resurrection, and the life" (John 11:25 KJV).

I remember a young girl in Boston, whose quiet, earnest testimony for Jesus drew people to our meetings just to hear her speak. One day, as we were walking along the street, she said to me, "The other evening, as I was in my room getting ready for the meeting, Jesus was with me. I felt He was there, and I knew Him."

I replied, "We may be more aware of His presence than of any earthly friend."

Then, to my surprise and joy, she said, "Yes, for He is in our hearts."

Paul had to be such a witness in order to bring salvation to the Gentiles. He was not a witness of the resurrection in the sense that he saw Jesus in the body with his natural eyes but in the higher, spiritual sense that "God . . . was pleased to reveal his Son" to Paul (Gal. 1:15–16 NIV)—and his testimony was just as mighty in convincing people of the truth and slaying their unbelief as was that of Peter or John.

And this power to witness was not confined to the apostles who had been with Jesus, and to Paul who was specially chosen to be an apostle; it is the common heritage of believers. Many years after Pentecost, Paul wrote to the Corinthians, far away in Europe, "Surely you know that Jesus Christ is among you" (2 Cor. 13:5 NLT). And, in writing to the Colossians, he said the mystery of the gospel is "Christ in you, the hope of glory" (Col. 1:27 KJV). In fact, this is the very highest purpose for which Jesus promised to send the Holy Spirit. He said, "When the Spirit of truth comes . . . he will not speak on his own. . . . He will bring me glory by telling you whatever he receives from me" (John 16:13–14 NLT).

This is the Holy Spirit's chief work—to reveal Jesus to the spiritual consciousness of each individual believer, and by so doing purify the heart, destroy all evil dispositions, and implant in the soul of the believer the very tempers and dispositions of Jesus Himself.

Indeed, the inward revelation of the mind and heart of Jesus through the baptism of the Holy Spirit was necessary in order to make fit witnesses out of the very men who had been with Him for three years and who were eyewitnesses of His death and resurrection.

Jesus did not rise from the dead and send His disciples out at once to tell the fact to everyone they met. He remained with them a few days, teaching them certain things, and then just before He ascended to heaven, instead of saying to them, "You have been with Me for three years, you know My life, you have heard My teachings, you saw Me die, you witnessed My resurrection—now go into all the world and tell them about these things," He commanded them, "Do not leave Jerusalem until the Father sends you the gift he promised, as I told you before. John baptized with water, but in just a few days you will be baptized with the Holy Spirit. . . . You will receive power when the Holy Spirit comes upon you. And you will be my witnesses" (Acts 1:4–5, 8 NLT).

The disciples had been with Jesus for three years, but they did not understand Him. He had been revealed to them in flesh and blood, but now He was to be revealed in them by the Spirit. And in that hour they knew His divinity and understood His character, His mission, His holiness, His everlasting love, and His saving power as they otherwise could not had He lived with them in the flesh to all eternity. This was what led Jesus to say to them, just before His death, "It is [better] for you that I go away: for if I go not away, the Comforter will not come unto you" (John 16:7 KJV). And if the Comforter had not come, they could not possibly have known Jesus except in the flesh.

Oh, how tenderly Jesus loved them, and with what unutterable longings did He wish to make Himself fully known to them! Just so today, does He want to make Himself fully known to His people and reveal Himself in their hearts. It is this knowledge of Jesus that skeptics and seekers want to see in Christians before they believe.

Now, if it is true that the children of God can so know Christ, that the Holy Spirit does so reveal Him, that Jesus does so earnestly wish to be known by His people, and that skeptics and seekers long to see evidence of in Christians before they will believe, is it not the duty of all followers of Jesus to seek Him wholeheartedly until they are filled with this knowledge and this power to witness? Further, this knowledge should be sought, not simply for usefulness, but for personal comfort and safety, because it is salvation—it is eternal life. Jesus said, "This is the way to have eternal life—to know you, the only true God, and Jesus Christ, the one you sent to earth" (John 17:3 NLT).

One may know ten thousand things about the Lord, may be very eloquent in speaking about His character and His works, and yet be utterly destitute of any heart acquaintance with Him. A peasant may know many things about an earthly ruler—may believe in his justice and be ready to trust his clemency, though he has never seen him—but it is his son and daughter and the members of his household who really know him. This universal revelation of the Lord Jesus is more than salvation—it is the positive side of that experience which we call a clean heart or "holiness." Do you want to know Him in this way? If your whole soul desires it, you may.

First, be sure your sins are forgiven. If you have wronged anybody, undo the wrong so far as you can. Zacchaeus said to Jesus, "I will give half my wealth to the poor, Lord, and if I have cheated people on their taxes, I will give them back four times as much!" (Luke 19:8 NLT), and Jesus saved him right on the spot. Submit to God, confess your sins, then trust Jesus, and as sure as you live all your sins shall be forgiven, and He will blot out all your transgressions as a thick cloud and remember them no more (see Jer. 31:34).

Second, now that you are forgiven, come to Him with your will, your affection, your very self, and ask Him to cleanse you from every evil temper, every selfish wish, every secret doubt; to come and dwell in your heart and keep you pure; and to use you for His own glory. Then struggle no more, but walk in the light He gives you and patiently, expectantly trust Him to answer your prayer. And as sure as you live you shall soon "be filled with all the fullness of God" (Eph. 3:19 KJV). At this point, do not become impatient and yield to secret doubts and fears, but "hold fast the profession of [your] faith" (Heb. 10:23 KJV) for, as the writer of Hebrews said, "Patient endurance is what you need now, so that you will continue to do God's will. Then you will receive all that he has promised" (Heb. 10:36–37 NLT). God will come to you! He will! And when He comes, He will satisfy the uttermost longings of your heart.

The Radicalism of Holiness

20

Do not think you can make holiness popular. It cannot be done. There is no such thing as holiness separate from "Christ in you" (Col. 1:27 KJV), and it is an impossibility to make Christ Jesus popular in this world. To the sinful and insincere, the real Christ Jesus has always been and always will be "like a root in dry ground . . . despised and rejected" (Isa. 53:2–3 NLT). "Christ in you" is "the same yesterday, today, and forever" (Heb. 13:8 NLT)—hated, reviled, persecuted, crucified.

"Christ in you" came not to send peace on earth, but a sword. He came "to set a man against his father, and a daughter against her mother, and a daughter-in-law against her mother-in-law" (Matt. 10:35–36 NLT).

"Christ in you" will not quench the smoking flax, nor break the bruised reed of penitence and humility (see Isa. 42:3), but He will pronounce the most terrible, yet tearful, maledictions against hypocritical formalists and lukewarm churchgoers who are the friends of the world and, consequently, the enemies of God. "Don't you realize that friendship with the world makes you an enemy of God? I say it again: If you want to be a friend of the world, you make yourself an enemy of God" (James 4:4 NLT). "When you love the world, you do not have the love of the Father in you" (1 John 2:15 NLT).

In the homes of the poor and the haunts of the outcast, "Christ in you" will seek and save the lost, and will sweetly, tenderly whisper, "Come to me . . . I will give you rest" (Matt. 11:28 NLT). But in stately church and cathedral, where pomp and pride and conformity to the world mock God, He will cry out with weeping and holy indignation, "I tell you the truth, corrupt tax collectors and prostitutes will get into the Kingdom of God before you do" (Matt. 21:31 NLT).

"Christ in you" is not a gorgeously robed aristocrat, arrayed in purple and fine linen and gold and pearls, but a lowly, peasant carpenter—a calloused, truth-telling, servant of servants, seeking always the lowest seat in the synagogues and at feasts, condescending to wash the feet of others. He "does not respect the proud" (Ps. 40:4 NKJV), nor is He like those who "flatter with their tongue" (Ps. 5:9 NKJV), but His words are "pure words, like silver refined in a furnace on the ground, purified seven times" (Ps. 12:6 ESV), words that are "living and powerful, and sharper than any two-edged sword . . . [discerning] the thoughts and intents of the heart" (Heb. 4:12 NKJV).

Seek to know and follow in the footsteps of the true, real Jesus, the humble, holy peasant of Galilee. For truly, many "false christs" as well as "false prophets" have gone out into the world.

There are dreamy, poetical christs, whose words are "soothing as lotion, but underneath are daggers" (Ps. 55:21 NLT). There are fashionable christs, "lovers of pleasure rather than lovers of God, having the appearance of godliness, but denying its power [holiness of heart]" (2 Tim. 3:4–5 ESV), who "work their way into people's homes and win the confidence of vulnerable women who are burdened with the guilt of sin and controlled by various desires . . . forever following new teachings, but . . . never able to understand the truth" (2 Tim. 3:6–7 NLT).

There are mercantile christs, who make God's house a den of thieves (see Matt. 21:13). There are feeding christs, who would catch people by feeding the stomach rather than the heart and head (see Rom. 16:18). There are learned, philosophical christs, who deceive people with "empty philosophies and high-sounding nonsense that come from human thinking" (Col. 2:8 NLT). There are political reform christs, who forget their Father's business in an all-absorbing effort to obtain power. They travel halfway across the continent to deliver a speech while a hundred thousand souls are going to hell at home and vainly endeavor to club the fruit off the branches rather than to lay the axe at the root of the tree, that the tree may be good (see Matt. 3:10).

They wanted to make Christ a king one day, but He wouldn't be a king, except of people's hearts. They wanted to make Him a judge one day for about five minutes, but He wouldn't be a judge. He made Himself of no reputation (see Phil. 2:7). He might have stopped on the throne of imperial Rome, or among the upper classes of society, or in the middle classes, but He went from His Father's bosom, down past the thrones and the upper, middle, and lower classes of society to the lowest place on earth and became a Servant of all, that He might lift us to the bosom of the Father and make us partakers of the divine nature and of His holiness (see 2 Pet. 1:4; Heb. 12:10).

"Christ in you" gets under men and women and lifts them up. If He had stopped on the throne, He never would have reached the poor fishermen of Galilee. But, going down among the fishermen, He soon shook earthly thrones.

It will not be popular, but "Christ in you" will go down. He will not seek the honor that comes from mere humans, but "the honor that comes from the only God" (John 5:44 NKJV; see also John 12:42–43).

One day a rich and influential young man came to Jesus and said, "Good Teacher, what must I do to inherit eternal life?" (Mark 10:17 NLT). This young man may have reasoned within himself, "The Master is poor, and I am rich. He will welcome me, for I can give Him financial prestige. The Master is without influence in the state, whereas I can give Him political power. The Master is under a social ban, associating with those poor, ignorant fishermen; I can give Him social influence."

But the Master struck at the heart of the man's worldly wisdom and self-conceit, and said, "Go and sell all your possessions and give the money to the poor. . . . Then come, follow me" (Mark 10:21 NLT). In other words, "Come, but you can serve Me only in poverty, in reproach, in humility, in social obscurity. For My kingdom is not of this world, and the weapons of this warfare are not carnal, but mighty through God to the pulling down of strongholds. You must deny your-self, for if you do not have My Spirit you do not belong to Me" (see John 18:36; 2 Cor. 10:4; Matt. 16:24; Rom. 8:9). He said, in effect,

"My spirit is one of self-sacrifice. You must give up your elegant Jerusalem home and come with Me. But remember, 'the Son of Man has no place even to lay his head' (Matt. 8:20 NLT). You will be considered little better than a common tramp. You must sacrifice your ease. You must give up your riches, for 'hasn't God chosen the poor in this world to be rich in faith? Aren't they the ones who will inherit the Kingdom?' (James 2:5 NLT). And it is easier for a camel to go through the eye of a needle than for a rich man to enter that kingdom (see Matt. 19:24). Remember, when you do this, you will lose your reputation. The bankers and belles of Jerusalem will say you are beside yourself, and your old friends will not acknowledge you when they meet you on the street. My heart is drawn to you; I love you (see Mark 10:21). But I tell you plainly that if you will not take up the cross and follow Me, you cannot be My disciple (see Luke 14:27). Indeed, 'if you want to be my disciple, you must hate everyone else by comparison—your father and mother, wife and children, brothers and sisters—yes, even your own life. Otherwise, you cannot be my disciple' (Luke 14:26 NLT). If you will do this, you shall have treasure in heaven (see Matt. 19:21)."

Do you not see the impossibility of making such a radical gospel as this popular? This Spirit and the spirit of the world are as fully opposed to each other as two locomotives on the same track running toward each other at the rate of sixty miles an hour. Fire and water will consort together as quickly as the "Christ in you" and the spirit of the world.

Do not waste your time trying to fix up a popular holiness. Just be holy because the Lord God is holy. Seek to please Him without regard to the likes or dislikes of others, and those who are disposed to be saved will soon see "Christ in you," and will cry out with Isaiah, "Woe is me! For I am lost; for I am a [person] of unclean lips, and I dwell in the midst of a people of unclean lips; for my eyes have seen the King, the LORD of hosts!" (Isa. 6:5 ESV). And, falling at His feet, they will say with the leper, "Lord, if you are willing, you can make me clean." And Jesus, having compassion on them, will say, "I am willing. . . . Be clean!" (Matt. 8:2–3 NIV).

Perfect Peace 21

"You will keep [us] in perfect peace" (Isa. 26:3 NLT). A wonderful promise is that, and it ought to be the aim of every one of us to make it our experience. The way to do this is simple: keep our minds fixed on our Lord. But while it is simple, I confess it is no easy matter for most people to do it. They would rather think about business, pleasure, politics, education, music, the news of the day, or even the work of the Lord than about the Lord Himself.

Now, business and other things must take some of our thought, and we must pay attention to the work of the Lord, if we love Him and the souls for whom He died. But just as the young bride filled with new cares is in her heart communing with her husband though he may be far from her, so we should in everything think of and commune with Jesus, and let our hearts fully trust His wisdom, love, and power. Then we shall be kept in perfect peace.

Just think of it! "All the treasures of wisdom and knowledge" are hid in Him, and we, in our ignorance and foolishness, are "complete in Him" (Col. 2:3, 10 KJV). We may not understand, but He understands. We may not know, but He knows. We may be perplexed, but He is not perplexed. Then we ought to trust Him if we are His, and we shall be kept in perfect peace.

Ten thousand times I have been at my wits' end, but oh, how it comforted me to know that Jesus saw the end from the beginning and was making all things work together for my good because I loved and trusted Him! Jesus is never at His wits' end. And when we are most puzzled and confounded by our foolishness and shortsightedness, Jesus is working out the desires of our hearts if they are holy desires— for does He not say, "He will fulfill the desire of them that fear him" (Ps. 145:19 KJV)?

Jesus not only has wisdom and love, but He assured us that "all power . . . in heaven and in earth" is His (Matt. 28:18 KJV), so that the counsels of His wisdom and the tender desire of His love cannot fail for lack of power to fulfill them. He can turn the hearts of kings and make them do His will, and His faithful love will lead Him to do it, if we will trust Him. Nothing is more surprising to the children of God who trust Him and watch His ways than the marvelous and unexpected deliverances He works out for them, and the kind of people He uses to fulfill His will.

Our hearts long to see the glory of the Lord and the prosperity of Zion, and we pray to God and wonder how the desire of our hearts is to be obtained. But we trust and look to God, and He sets to work, with the most unlikely people and in the most unheard of way, to answer our prayers and reward our patient faith. And so, in all the little vexatious trials and delays of our everyday, plodding life, if we trust and keep on rejoicing right through all that bothers us, we will find God at work for us, for He says He is a "present help in trouble" (Ps. 46:1 KJV)—all trouble—and so He is to all who keep their minds stayed on Him.

Only a short period has elapsed since the Lord has been allowing me to pass through a series of the most troublesome times, just calculated to annoy me to the uttermost. But while waiting on Him in prayer, He showed me that if I had more confidence in Him in my difficulties, I would keep on rejoicing and so get blessings out of my trials as Samson got honey out of the carcass of the lion he slew. And so I proved it to be. I did rejoice, and one trial after the other vanished away. Only the sweetness of my Lord's presence and blessing remained, and my heart has been kept in perfect peace since.

Does not God do all this to remove pride from us, to humble us and make us see that our character before Him is of more consequence than our service to Him? Does He not do it to teach us to walk by faith and not by sight and to encourage us to trust and be at peace?

Now, let no honest soul whose faith is small—nor busybodies who seem to think that if they did not worry and fret and rush about and make a great noise the universe would come to a standstill and go to ruin—suppose for an instant that there is any likeness whatever between perfect peace and perfect indifference. Indifference is a child of sloth. Peace is the offspring of a faith that is ceaseless in its activity— an activity that is the most perfect and the mightiest of which human beings are capable, for through it poor, unarmed people have "subdued kingdoms, wrought righteousness, obtained promises, stopped the mouths of lions, quenched the violence of fire, escaped the edge of the sword, out of weakness were made strong, waxed valiant in fight, turned to flight the armies of the aliens, [and] women received their dead raised to life again" (Heb. 11:33–35 KJV).

To exercise this mighty faith which brings perfect peace, we must receive the Holy Spirit into our hearts and recognize Him not as an influence or an attribute of God, but as God Himself. He is a person, and He will make us know Jesus, understand His mind and will, and realize His constant presence, if we trust Him. Jesus is ever present with us, and if we long for Him, it will so please Him that He will always help us to fix our minds on Him.

It will require some effort on our part, however, for the world, our business, the weakness of the flesh, the infirmities of our minds, the careless example of the people about us, and the Devil with all his wiles will so seek to turn our thoughts from our Lord and make us forget Him that maybe not more than once or twice in twenty-four hours shall our thoughts and affections turn to Him. And it will happen only by a strong and prolonged effort, so that even in times of prayer we may not really find God.

Let us then cultivate the habit of communing with Jesus. When our thoughts wander from Him, let us turn them back again. But let us do this quietly and patiently, for any impatience—even with ourselves— is dangerous, disturbing our inward peace, drowning the still, small voice of the Spirit and hindering the grace of God from mastering us and subduing our hearts.

But if, in all meekness and lowliness of heart, we allow the Holy Spirit to dwell in us and are obedient to His voice, He will keep our hearts in a holy calm in the midst of ten thousand cares and weaknesses and troubles.

"Don't worry about anything; instead, pray about everything. Tell God what you need, and thank him for all he has done. Then you will experience God's peace, which exceeds anything we can understand. His peace will guard your hearts and minds as you live in Christ Jesus" (Phil. 4:6–7 NLT).

Some of My Experiences in Teaching Holiness

I once received a letter from one of the most devoted young Salvation Army officers I know, in which he said, "I love holiness more and more, but I am just about discouraged. It seems to me that I shall never be able to teach holiness, for it seems that I get things too straight, or not straight enough." I think I know just how he feels. One day, a few months after I received the blessing of holiness, I felt most gloomy about my inability to get people sanctified. I knew, beyond the possibility of a doubt, that I had a clean heart, but somehow I felt I couldn't properly teach others how to get it.

That morning I met a certain brother who gets more people sanctified than anyone I know, and I asked him, "How shall I teach holiness so that my people will get it?" His reply was, "Load and fire, load and fire."

Light broke in on me at once. I saw that it was my business to pray and study my Bible and talk with those who had the blessing until I got myself so loaded that it would almost talk itself, and then fire away as best I could. And I saw that it was God's business to make the people receive the truth and become holy.

That was on a Saturday. The next day, I went to my people loaded with truth, backed by love and faith, and I fired as hard and straight as I knew how, and twenty people came to the penitent form seeking holiness. I had never seen anything like that before in my life, but I have seen it many times since.

From then till now I have attended strictly to my part of the business and trusted God to do His part, and I have had some success everywhere I have gone. But everywhere, also, Satan has sorely tempted me at times, especially when people hardened their hearts and would not believe and obey. Then I have often felt that the trouble must be in my way of preaching the truth. At one time the Devil would say, "You are too straight; you will drive all the people away." Then again he would remark, "You are not straight enough, and that is the reason the people don't get holy." In this way, I have suffered very much at times. But I have always gone to the Lord with my trouble and told Him that He knew my earnest desire was to preach the truth just right, so that the people would love and trust Him with perfect hearts.

Then the Lord has comforted me and shown me that the Devil was tempting me in order to get me to stop preaching holiness. A few times, so-called Christians have come to me and told me I was doing more harm than good. But they were the kind Paul described, who "act religious, but . . . reject the power that could make them godly" and I have followed his command, "Stay away from people like that" (2 Tim. 3:5 NLT). I have not dared to listen to them any more than to the Devil himself. So I have kept at it, through evil report and through good report, and the dear Lord has never left me alone but has stood by me and given me the victory, and I have repeatedly seen someone led into the glorious light of liberty and perfect love. Satan has tried in many ways to get me to stop preaching holiness, for he knew that if he could get me to stop, he would soon get me to sin and so overthrow me altogether. But the Lord put a godly fear in me from the beginning by calling my attention to the words of Jeremiah: "'O Sovereign LORD,' I said, 'I can't speak for you!'" The Lord replied, "Do not be afraid of the people, for I will be with you and will protect you. I, the LORD, have spoken!" (Jer. 1:6, 8 NLT).

"Get up and prepare for action. Go out and tell them everything I tell you to say. Do not be afraid of them, or I will make you look foolish in front of them" (Jer. 1:17 NLT). That last verse made me very careful to speak just what the Lord said. Then the words of Ezekiel impressed me very much:

> They are a stubborn and hard-hearted people. But I am sending you to say to them, "This is what the Sovereign LORD says!" And whether they listen or refuse to listen—for remember, they are rebels—at least they will know they have had a prophet among them. "Son of man, do not fear them or their words. Don't be afraid even though their threats surround you like nettles and briers and stinging scorpions. Do not be dismayed by their dark scowls, even though they are rebels. You must give them my messages whether they listen or not. But they won't listen, for they are completely rebellious! Son of man,

listen to what I say to you. Do not join them in their rebellion. Open your mouth, and eat what I give you." . . . But look, I have made you as obstinate and hard-hearted as they are. I have made your forehead as hard as the hardest rock! So don't be afraid of them or fear their angry looks, even though they are rebels." Then he added, "Son of man, let all my words sink deep into your own heart first. Listen to them carefully for yourself. Then go to your people in exile and say to them, 'This is what the Sovereign LORD says!' Do this whether they listen to you or not." (Ezek. 2:4–8; 3:8–11 NLT)

In these Scriptures, the Lord commanded me to speak His truth as He gave it to me, whether the people would hear or not. And in Ephesians 4:15, He told me how I was to preach it—in love. I then saw that I must preach the truth just as straight as I possibly could, but that I must be careful always to keep my heart full of love for the people to whom I was talking.

I read in 2 Corinthians how Paul loved the people. He said, "I don't want what you have—I want you. . . . I will gladly spend myself and all I have for you, even though it seems that the more I love you, the less you love me" (2 Cor. 12:14–15 NLT). Then in Acts, he said, "I never shrank back from telling you what you needed to hear. . . . I didn't shrink from declaring all that God wants you to know" (Acts 20:20, 27 NLT). This made me feel that to withhold the truth of holiness from the people—which is necessary to their eternal salvation—was worse than keeping back bread from starving children, as the murder of souls is even worse than the murder of bodies. So I earnestly prayed to the Lord to help me love the people and preach the whole truth to them, though they hate me for it—and He answered my prayer.

There are three points in teaching holiness that the Lord has led me to emphasize continually. First, that men and women cannot make themselves holy, any more than the leopard can change its spots. No amount of good works can cleanse the heart and take out the roots of pride, vanity, temper, impatience, lust, hatred, strife, self-indulgence, and the like, and in their stead put perfect love, peace, longsuffering, gentleness, goodness, faith, meekness, and temperance. Truly, millions who have labored to purify the secret springs of their hearts, only to fail, can testify, "It is 'not a result of works, so that no one may boast'" (Eph. 2:9 ESV).

Second, I keep prominent the fact that the blessing is received by faith. A poor woman wanted some grapes from the king's garden for her sick boy. She offered the gardener money, but he would not sell the grapes. She came again, met the king's daughter, and offered her money for the grapes. The daughter said, "My father is a king; he does not sell his grapes." Then she led the poor woman into the king's presence and told him her story, and he gave her as many as she wanted.

Our God, your Father, is King of Kings. He will not sell His holiness and the graces of His Spirit, but He will give them to all who will ask in simple, childlike faith. "Ask and it will be given to you" (Matt. 7:7 NIV). "Can we boast, then, that we have done anything to be accepted by God? No, because our acquittal is not based on obeying the law. It is based on faith" (Rom. 3:27 NLT). The apostle Paul said, "It is by believing in your heart that you are made right with God" (Rom. 10:10 NLT), and that statement is true to our experience, for where real heart faith is, it makes the impatient person patient, the proud humble, the lustful chaste, the covetous generous, the quarrelsome meek, the liar truthful, the hateful loving, and turns misery into joy and gives peace and constant comfort.

Third, I emphasize the truth that the blessing is to be received by faith *now*. The person who expects to get it by works will always have something more to do before claiming the blessing, and so never comes to the point where he or she can say, "The blessing is now mine." But the humble soul, who expects to get it by faith, sees that it is a gift and, believing that God is as willing to give it now as at some future time, trusts and receives it at once.

By thus urging the people to expect the blessing right now, I have sometimes had them get it even as I was talking. People who had often been to the penitent form and had wrestled and prayed for the blessing have received it while sitting in their seats listening to the simple "word of faith, which we preach" (Rom. 10:8 KJV).

Another Chance for You! 23

Peter vowed before his comrades that he would die with Jesus rather than deny Him. A few hours later the opportunity to do so presented itself, but Peter's heart failed him. He forgot his vow and threw away forever this unparalleled chance of proving his love for the Savior.

When the cock crowed and Jesus turned and looked at him, Peter remembered his broken vow and went out and wept bitterly. The tenderest sorrow for the way he had treated Jesus must have mingled with the fiercest regret for the lost chance for those bitter tears to appear. Oh, how his love must have reproached him, his conscience stung him, and the Devil taunted him! I doubt not he was tempted to give up all hope and said to himself, "It is of no use for me to try to be a Christian; I have made a miserable failure, and I will not try any longer." And over and over again, by day and by night, in the company of others and when by himself, Peter must have been reminded by the Devil of his lost chance and told it was no use for him to try any longer to be a Christian. And I imagine Peter sighed within himself and would have given the world to have that chance come back once more. But it was gone, and gone forever!

Peter did love Jesus, however, and while he had lost that chance to demonstrate his love, Jesus gave him another. A very simple, everyday, matter-of-fact chance it was, nothing like the startling, splendid one of dying with the Son of God on the cross, but probably of far more value to the world and the cause of Christ. All over the country where Jesus had been, there were, doubtless, many who believed with a trembling faith in Him. They needed to be faithfully fed with the truths about Jesus, and with those truths He had taught. So Jesus called Peter to Him and asked him three times the searching question: "Do you love me?" (John 21:15–17 NIV). It must have most painfully recalled to Peter's mind the three times he had denied Jesus. And in reply to Peter's positive assertion that he did love Him, Jesus three times commanded him to feed His lambs and sheep. And then Jesus assured Peter that at last he should die on a cross—as he probably would have died had he not denied his Lord.

I suspect there are many Peters among the disciples of Jesus today—many in our own ranks, who, somewhere in the past, since they began to follow Jesus, vowed they would do the thing He by His Spirit through their conscience asked them to do, vowed they would die for Him (and meant it, too); who, when the testing time came, forgot their vows, denied Jesus by word or act, and practically left Him to be crucified afresh and alone.

I remember a time when I failed my Lord, years ago, before I joined The Salvation Army but after I was sanctified. It was not a sin of commission, but one of omission—a failure to do what I felt the Lord would have me do. It was an unusual thing, but not an unreasonable one. The suggestion to act came suddenly, and it seemed to me that all heaven bent over me to bless me if I obeyed and hell yawned to swallow me if I did not. I did not say I would not, but it seemed to me I simply could not—and I did not. Oh, how I was humbled! I wept bitter tears, begged forgiveness, and promised God I would be true! I felt God had given me a chance that I had let slip by and that would never come again, and that I could never be the mighty man of faith and obedience I might have been had I been true. Then I promised God that I would do that very same thing, and I did it again and again, but no real blessing came to me, and so Satan took advantage of me and taunted me and accused me through my conscience till life became an intolerable burden to me. At last I felt I had grieved the Holy Spirit forever and that I was lost, and so I threw away my shield of faith, cast away my confidence in the love of Jesus for me, and for twenty-eight days suffered, it seemed to me, the pains of hell. I still prayed, but the heavens were like brass to me. I read my Bible, but the promises fled away from me, while the commandments and warnings were like flames of fire and two-edged swords to my quivering conscience. When it was night I longed for day; when it was day I longed for night.

I went to worship meetings, but no blessing came to me. The curse of God seemed to follow me, and yet through it all I saw that God is love. Satan tempted me to commit sin, to curse God and die, as Job's wife urged him. But God's mercy and grace followed me and enabled me to say no, and to tell the Devil that I would not sin and that though I went to hell, I would go there loving Jesus and seeking to get others to trust and obey Him, and that in hell I would declare that the blood of Jesus could cleanse from all sin. I thought I was doomed. Those terrible passages of Scripture in Hebrews 6 and 10 seemed just to fit my case, and I said, "I have lost my chance forever." But God's love is "higher than the highest heaven, deeper than the deepest sea."[1]

In twenty-eight days, He drew me up out of that horrible pit and that miry clay with these words: "Hold it for certain that all such thoughts as create disquiet proceed not from God, who is the Prince of Peace, but proceed either from the Devil, or from self-love, or from the good opinion we hold of ourselves."[2]

Quick as thought I saw it: God is the Prince of Peace. His thoughts are "thoughts of peace, and not of evil" (Jer. 29:11 KJV). I saw I had no self-love, nor good opinion of myself, and longed to be forever rid of self. Then I saw that the Devil was deceiving me, and instantly it was as though a devil loosened his long arms from about my spirit and fled away, leaving me free.

The next Saturday and Sunday I saw about fifty souls at the penitent form seeking salvation and holiness, and from that hour God has blessed me and given me souls everywhere. He has asked me, through those words He spoke to Peter, "Do you love Me?" And when, out of the fullness of my clean heart—emptied of self and made clean through His precious blood—I have said, "Lord, You know everything; You know that I love You," He has tenderly bidden me to feed His lambs and sheep—that is, to live the gospel so fully in my life and preach it so fully in my words that His people will be blessed, comforted, and encouraged to love and serve and trust Him with all their hearts.

This is my "second chance," and it can be yours, even if you have denied Him in the past.

Do not seek to do some great thing, but feed the lambs and sheep of God, and pray and work for the salvation of others. Study your Bible, pray, talk often and much with God, and ask Him to teach you so that, whenever you open your mouth, you may say something that will bless somebody, something that will encourage a discouraged brother or sister, strengthen a weak one, instruct an ignorant one, comfort a feeble-minded one, warn an erring one, enlighten a darkened one, and rebuke a sinning one.

Notice that Peter was to feed not only the lambs, but also the sheep. We must help others experience new life in Christ and, after they are "born again," we must feed them. We must feed the new Christians on those promises and instructions in God's Word that will lead them into entire sanctification. We must show them that this is God's will for them and that Jesus has opened a way for them "to enter into the holiest" (Heb. 10:19 KJV). We must warn them not to turn back into Egypt, not to be afraid of the giants in the Promised Land, nor to make any unholy alliance with the Ammonites in the wilderness. They are to come out and be separate. They are to be holy. This is their high and happy privilege and their solemn duty, since they have been redeemed, not with corruptible things such as silver and gold, but with the precious blood of Christ (see 1 Pet. 1:18–19). They are not to faint when chastened and corrected by the Lord, nor grow weary in doing good (see Gal. 6:9).

They are to watch and pray and give thanks and rejoice always. And they are not to get the blessing of a clean heart by hard work, nor only in the hour of death, but by simple faith in Jesus right now.

We must feed the sheep, the sanctified ones, on the strong meat of the gospel. Feed a strong man on white bread and tea, and he will soon be unfit for work. But give him good brown bread, butter and milk, and suitable fruits and vegetables, and the harder he works, other things being equal, the better he is in health and strength. So it is with Christians. Feed them on the chaff of stale jokes and last year's Bible readings that have lost their power on your own heart, and you will starve the sheep. But feed them on the deep things of God's Word, which reveal His everlasting love, His faithfulness, His saving power, His tender and attentive care, His shining holiness, His exact justice, His hatred of sin, His pity for the sinner, His sympathy for the weak and erring, His eternal judgments upon the finally impenitent and ungodly, and His never-ending glory and blessedness bestowed upon the righteous, and you will make them so strong that "one [shall] chase a thousand, and two put ten thousand to flight" (Deut. 32:30 KJV).

Know Jesus, and you will be able to feed His lambs and sheep. You feed them by revealing Him to them as He is revealed by the Father through the Spirit in the Bible.

Walk with Him. Talk with Him. Search the Bible on your knees, asking Him to open your understanding as He did that of the disciples on the way to Emmaus, teaching you what the Scriptures say of Him, and you will have another chance of showing your love for Him and of blessing others that the angels might well covet.

NOTES

1. Theodore Monod, "O, the Bitter Shame and Sorrow," 1874, public domain.

2. St. *Francis de Sales, Jane de Chantal, Letters of Spiritual Direction*, The Classics of Western Spirituality (Mahway, NJ: Paulist Press, 1988), 51.

Birds of Prey 24

Satan brings to bear all his devices—his sophisticated arguments and the full force of his powerful will—against the entire sanctification of believers. But the resolute soul, determined to be all the Lord's, will find him a conquered foe with no power except to deceive. The way to overcome him is to decide to steadfastly believe and agree with God, in spite of all Satan's suggested doubts.

In the fifteenth chapter of Genesis, we have an account of Abraham's sacrifice, which is very suggestive to the seeker after full salvation. Abraham took certain beasts and birds and offered them to God. But after he had made the offering and while he was waiting for the witness of God's acceptance, birds of prey came to snatch away the sacrifice. Abraham drove them away. This continued until the evening, and then the fire of God consumed the offering.

Just so, the person who would be entirely sanctified must make an unreserved offering of him- or herself to God. This act must be real, not imaginary—a real transfer of self, with all hopes, plans, prospects, property, cares, burdens, joys, sorrows, reputation, and friends to God in a "perpetual covenant that shall not be forgotten" (Jer. 50:5 KJV). When we have thus given ourselves to God, we must, like Abraham, patiently, trustingly, expectantly wait for God to witness that we are accepted. "If it seems slow in coming, wait patiently, for it will surely take place. It will not be delayed" (Hab. 2:3 NLT).

Now, during this period of waiting, the Devil will surely send his birds of prey to snatch away the offering. He will say, "You ought to feel different if you have given yourself wholly to God." Remember, that is the Devil's bird of prey—drive it away. Feelings are an effect, not a cause. To have the feeling of love, I must think of some loved one. But the very moment I get my thought off the object of my love and examine my feelings, they begin to subside. Look to Jesus and pay no attention to your emotions. They are involuntary, but will soon adjust themselves to the fixed habit of your faith and will.

"But," something suggests, "maybe your consecration is not complete; go over it again and be sure." Another bird of prey—drive it away.

Satan becomes extremely pious at this point and wants to keep you eternally on the treadmill of consecration, knowing that as long as he can keep you examining your consecration, you will not get your eyes on the promise of God and, consequently, will not believe. Thus, without faith that your offering is accepted, it is only so much dead works.

"But you do not have the joy, the deep and powerful emotions that others say they have." That is another bird of prey—drive it away.

A woman recently said to me, "I have given up all, but I have not the happiness I expected."

"Ah, sister," I said, "the promise is not unto them who seek happiness, but to them 'which hunger and thirst after righteousness, they shall be filled.' Seek righteousness, not happiness."

She did so, and in a few moments she was satisfied, for with righteousness came fullness of joy.

"But faith is such an incomprehensible something, you cannot exercise it. Pray to God to help your unbelief." The Devil's bird of prey—drive it away.

Faith is almost too simple to be defined. It is trust in the word of Jesus, simple confidence that He means just what He says in all the promises and that He means all the promises for you. Beware of being "corrupted from the simplicity that is in Christ" (2 Cor. 11:3 KJV).

I tell you, dear friend, everything contrary to present faith in the promise of God for full salvation is one of the Devil's birds of prey, and you must resolutely drive it away.

Quit reasoning with the Devil! "Demolish arguments and every pretension that sets itself up against the knowledge of God" (2 Cor. 10:5 NIV) and trust. Reason with God. "'Come now, and let us reason together,' says the LORD" (Isa. 1:18 NKJV).

At one of our watchnight services, a man knelt with quite a number of others, seeking a clean heart. He was told to give himself wholly to God and trust. Finally, he began to pray, and then he said, "I do give myself to God, and now I am going to live and work for

Him with what power I have and let Him give me the fullness of the blessing and power just when He chooses. He has promised to give it to me, and He will do it, will He not?"

"Yes, my brother," I replied. "He has promised, and He will surely perform."

"Yes, yes; He had promised it," said the man. Just then light shot through his soul, and his next words were, "Praise the Lord! Glory to God!" He reasoned together with God and, looking to the promise, was delivered. Others around him reasoned with the Devil, looked to their feelings, and were not sanctified.

But after you have taken the step of faith, God's plan is for you to talk your faith. The men and women of character, of force and influence, are those who put themselves on record. The one who has convictions, and who is not afraid to announce them to the world and defend them, is the one who has true stability. It is so in politics, in business, in all moral reforms, and in salvation. There is a universal law underlying the declaration: "With the mouth confession is made unto salvation" (Rom. 10:10 KJV). If you are sanctified and would remain sanctified, you must at the earliest opportunity put yourself on record before all the devils in hell, all your acquaintances on earth, and all the angels in heaven. You must stand before the world as a professor and possessor of heart purity. Only in this way can you burn all the bridges behind you. Until they are destroyed, you are not safe.

A woman said to me, "I have always hesitated to say, 'The Lord sanctifies me wholly,' but not until recently did I see the reason. I now see that I secretly desired a bridge behind me, so that I might escape back from my position without injury to myself. If I profess sanctification, I must be careful lest I bring myself into disrepute. But if I do not profess it, I can do questionable things and then shield myself by saying, 'I do not profess to be perfect.'"

Ah, that is the secret! Be careful not to become a religious fence rider, for all who are astride the fence are really on the Devil's side. "Whoever that is not with me is against me" (Matt. 12:30 NIV). Get onto God's side by a definite profession of your faith.

But the Devil will say, "You had better not say anything about this till you find out whether you will be able to keep it. Be careful, lest you do more harm than good." Drive that bird of prey away quickly or all you have done thus far will be of no avail. That bird has devoured tens of thousands of offerings just as honestly made as yours. You are not to "keep the blessing" at all; you are to boldly assert your faith in the Blesser, and He will keep you.

A brother said to me, "When I sought this experience, I gave myself definitely and fully to God and told Him I would trust Him; but I felt as dry as that post. Shortly after this, a friend asked me if I were sanctified, and before I had time to examine my feelings, I said 'Yes.' And God that minute blessed me and filled me full of His Spirit, and since then He has sweetly kept me."

He talked his faith and agreed with God.

"But you want to be honest and not claim more than you possess," says Satan. A bird of prey!

You must assert that you believe God to be honest and that He has promised that "whatever you ask in prayer, believe that you have received it, and it will be yours" (Mark 11:24 ESV). Count God faithful.

An acquaintance of mine gave herself to God, but did not feel any difference, and so hesitated to say that God had sanctified her wholly.

"But," she said, "I began to reason over the matter thus: I know I have given myself wholly to God. I am willing to be anything, do anything, suffer anything for Jesus. I am willing to forego all pleasure, honor, and all my cherished hopes and plans for His sake, but I do not feel that God sanctifies me. And yet He promises to do so on the simple condition that I give myself to Him and believe His Word. Knowing that I have given myself to Him, I must believe or make Him a liar; so I will believe that He does now sanctify me. But," she continued, "I did not get any witness that the work was done just then. However, I rested in God, and some days after this I went to one of the holiness conventions, and there, while a number were testifying, I thought I would rise and tell them God sanctified me. I did so, and between rising up and sitting down, God came and witnessed that it was done. Now I know I am sanctified."

And her shining face was a sufficient evidence that the work was indeed done.

"Resist the devil, and he will flee from you" (James 4:7 KJV). Give yourself wholly to God, trust Him, and then confess your faith. "'Then the LORD you are seeking will suddenly come to His temple. The messenger of the covenant, whom you look for so eagerly, is surely coming,' says the LORD of Heaven's Armies" (Mal. 3:1 NLT).

With Peace Unbroken 25

The Reverend John Fletcher, whom Wesley thought was the holiest man who had lived since the days of the apostle John, lost the blessing five times before he was finally established in the grace of holiness, and Wesley declared that he was persuaded, from his observations, that people usually lose the blessing several times before they learn the secret of keeping it. So, if you have lost the blessing and are tormented by the old Enemy of souls—the Devil—with the thought that you can never get and keep it, let me urge you to try again and again.

You prove your real desire and purpose to be holy, not by giving up in the presence of defeat, but by rising from ten thousand falls and going at it again with renewed faith and consecration. If you do this, you shall surely win the prize and be able to keep it in the end.

The promise is: "Seek and you will find" (Matt. 7:7 NIV).

"But how long shall I seek?"

Seek till you find!

"But suppose I lose it?"

God will surprise you someday by pouring out such a full baptism of His Spirit upon you, that all your darkness and doubts and uncertainty will vanish forever, you will never fall again, God's smile will no more be withdrawn, and your sun will nevermore go down.

Oh, let me urge you to look up and trust Jesus, and keep on seeking, remembering that God's delays are not denial—Jesus is your Joshua to lead you into the Promised Land, and He can cast down all your foes before you. People who give up in the midst of defeat have much to learn of the deceitfulness and hardness of their own hearts, and of the tender forbearance, longsuffering, and mighty saving power of God. But it is not God's will that any who receive the blessing should ever lose it, and it is possible to keep it forever.

But how?

One day, as an old divinity school chum of mine, who had finished his course of study, was going to his field of labor, I followed him to the train to have a hearty handshake and to say good-bye, perhaps forever. He looked up and said, "Sam, give me a text that will do for a life motto."

Instantly I lifted my heart to God for light. Now, if you want to keep the blessing, that is one of the things you must constantly do—lift your heart to God and look to Him for light, not only in the crises and great events of life, but in all its little and seemingly trifling details. By practice, you can get into such a habit of doing this that it will become as natural for you as breathing, and it will prove quite as important to your spiritual life as breathing is to your natural life. Keep within whispering distance of God always, if you would keep the blessing. Well, I proved to be in whisper touch with Jesus that morning on the train. Immediately the first eleven verses of the first chapter of 2 Peter were suggested to my mind—not simply as a motto, but as a plain rule laid down by the Holy Spirit which, by following we may not only keep the blessing and never fall, but also prove fruitful in the knowledge of God and gain an abundant entrance into the kingdom of our Lord and Savior Jesus Christ.

Notice it, if you wish to keep the blessing of holiness. The apostle spoke of being made "partakers of the divine nature, having escaped from the corruption that is in the world because of sinful desire" (2 Pet. 1:4 ESV). That is holiness: to escape from the corruption of our evil hearts and receive the divine nature. And in verse 5 the apostle urged these holy people to diligence, and not only diligence, but "all diligence" (KJV). To keep the blessing you must use all diligence.

A lazy, sleepy man or woman cannot keep the blessing; in fact, such a person cannot get it in the first place. To get it you must seek it with all your heart. You must dig as for hidden treasure, and to keep it you must use diligence. Some people say, "Once saved, always saved," but God does not say anything of the kind. He urges us to watch and be sober and diligent, for we are in the Enemy's country. This world is not a friend to grace. If you had one hundred thousand dollars' worth of diamonds in a land of robbers, you would watch and keep your treasure with all diligence. Well, you are in the Enemy's country, with a holy heart and "the Spirit as a deposit" (2 Cor. 1:22; 5:5 NIV), your passport to heaven, your pledge of eternal life. Be diligent to keep it.

The apostle Peter said, "Beside this, giving all diligence, add to your faith virtue" (2 Pet. 1:5 KJV). You had to have faith in "the exceeding great and precious promises" (2 Pet. 1:4 KJV) to get this blessing, but you will have to add something more to your faith to keep it. This word *virtue* comes from the old Latin word which means "courage," and that is probably its meaning here. You must have courage to keep this blessing.

The Devil will roar like a lion at you at times. The world will frown upon you, and maybe beat you up and possibly kill you. Your friends will pity you, or curse you, and predict all sorts of calamities as sure to befall you. At times, even your own flesh may cry out against you. Then you will need courage.

They told me I would go crazy, and it almost seemed that I would, so earnest was I to know all the mind of God for me. They said I would land in a bog of fanaticism. They said I would end in the poorhouse. They said I would utterly ruin my health and become a lifelong, useless invalid, a torment to myself and a burden to my friends. The very bishop whose book on holiness had stirred my soul to its depths urged me after I got the blessing to say very little about it, as it caused much division and trouble. (I afterward learned that he had lost the blessing.) The Devil followed me day and night with a thousand spiritual temptations I had never dreamed of, and then at last stirred up a thug to nearly knock my brains out. For many months I was prostrated with bodily weakness until the writing of a postcard plunged me into distress and robbed me of a night's rest. So I found it took courage to keep this pearl of great price. But the Lion of the tribe of Judah, who is my Lord and Savior, is as full of courage as He is of strength and love and pity, and He has said in the Book of instruction and encouragement He has left us, "Be strong and courageous" (Josh. 1:6 NLT). He put it even stronger and said, "This is my *command*—be strong and courageous!" (Josh. 1:9 NLT, emphasis added). It is a positive command, which we are under obligation to obey. Over and over again He said this, and seventy-two times He said, "Don't be afraid." And He added, as a sufficient reason why we should not fear, "For I am with you" (Isa. 41:10 NLT). If He is with me, why should I be afraid? And why should you?

My little boy is very much afraid of dogs, as if this fear was born in him. But when he gets hold of my hand he will march boldly past the biggest dog in the country. God says, "For I, the LORD your God, hold your right hand; it is I who say to you, 'Fear not, I am the one who helps you. . . . Fear not, for I am with you; be not dismayed, for I am your God; I will strengthen you, I will help you, I will uphold you with my righteous right hand'" (Isa. 41:13, 10 ESV).

"Never will I leave you," He says. "Never will I forsake you" (Heb. 13:5 NIV). Never! Jesus, the very same Jesus who died for us, says, "I have been given all authority in heaven and on earth. . . . And be sure of this: I am with you always, even to the end of the age" (Matt. 28:18, 20 NLT). Why fear?

The Devil is an old hand at deceiving and overthrowing souls, but remember that Jesus is the Ancient of Days. From everlasting to everlasting, He is God, and He has put all the wisdom and power and courage of His Godhead at the disposal of our faith for our salvation. Certainly that ought to fill us with courage. Are you downhearted and afraid? Cheer up! Pluck up courage, and let us boldly say with King

David, who had a good deal more trouble and cause for fear than we do: "God is our refuge and strength, always ready to help in times of trouble. So we will not fear when earthquakes come and the mountains crumble into the sea" (Ps. 46:1–2 NLT).

I have been helped very much by one experience of David's. On one occasion he had to flee from Saul, who hunted for his life as men hunt for partridges on the mountains. So David went down into Philistia and dwelt in a village that the king gave him. Then the Philistines went to war against Saul, and David went too. But they were afraid David might turn against them in the hour of battle, so they sent him home. When David and his men returned to their homes, they found some enemies had been there, had burned their village to the ground, and had carried off their goods, cattle, wives, and children. The men were mad with grief and determined to stone David. Certainly there was reason for fear. But the Bible says, "David encouraged himself in the LORD" (1 Sam. 30:6 KJV). Read the story for yourself, and see how wonderfully God helped him to get everything back again (see 1 Sam. 30).

As for me, I am determined to be of good courage. God has been better to me than all my fears and the fears of all my friends. He has outwitted all my enemies and proved stronger than all my foes. And He has enabled me, by His power and infinite love and goodness, to walk in holiness before Him for many years.

Sanctification versus Consecration 26

A state senator's wife regularly attended a series of our holiness meetings. One day she came to me and said, "Brother Brengle, I wish you would call it 'consecration' instead of 'sanctification.' We could all agree on that."

I replied, "But I don't mean consecration, sister. I mean sanctification, and there is as big a difference between the two as there is between earth and heaven, between our work and God's work."

Her mistake is a common one. She wanted to rob holiness of its supernatural element and rest in her own works. It is more fashionable to be consecrated and to talk much about consecration. Lovely ladies, robed in silk and bedecked with jewels, feathers, and flowers, and gentlemen with soft hands and suits and odorous with perfume, talk with honeyed words and sweet, low voices about being consecrated to the Lord.

And I would not discourage them, but I do want to lift up my voice with a loud warning that consecration, as such people ordinarily think of it, is simply our work, and is not enough to save the soul.

Elijah piled his altar on Mount Carmel, slew his bullock and placed it on the altar, and then poured water over the whole. That was consecration.

But Baal's priests had done that, with the exception of putting on the water. They had built their altar and slain their bullocks. They had spent the day in the most earnest religious devotions and, so far as everyone could see, their zeal far exceeded that of Elijah.

What did Elijah do more than they? Nothing, except to pour water on his sacrifice—a big venture of faith. If he had stopped there, the world would never have heard of him. But he believed for *God* to do something. He expected it, he prayed for it, and God split the heavens and poured down fire to consume his sacrifice, the stones of his altar, and the very water that lay in the trenches. That was sanctification!

What power had cold stones and water and a dead bullock to glorify God and convert an apostate nation? But when they were flaming, and being consumed with the fire from heaven, then "they fell face down on the ground and cried out, 'The LORD—he is God! Yes, the LORD is God!'" (1 Kings 18:39 NLT).

What do great gifts and talk and so-called consecration amount to in saving the world and glorifying God? "If I give all my possessions to feed the poor, and if I surrender my body to be burned, but do not have love, it profits me nothing" (1 Cor. 13:3 NASB). It is God in us that enables us to glorify Him and work together with Him for the salvation of the world.

God wants sanctified men and women. Of course, we must be consecrated—that is, given up to God—in order to be sanctified. But once we have yielded ourselves to Him—yielded our very inmost selves, our memories, our minds and wills, our tongues, our hands and feet, our reputations, our doubts and fears, our likes and dislikes, and our disposition to talk back at God and pity ourselves and murmur and repine when He puts our consecration to the test—when we have really done this and taken our hands off, as Elijah placed his bullock on the altar and took his hands off, then we must wait on God and cry to Him with a humble, yet bold, persistent faith until He baptizes us with the Holy Spirit and fire. He promised to do it, and He will do it, but we must expect it, pray for it, and if it delays, wait for it.

A soldier (church member) went home from one of our meetings, fell on his knees, and said, "Lord, I will not get up from here till you baptize me with the Holy Ghost!" God saw He had a man on his hands who meant business, who wanted God more than all creation, and so He there and then baptized the man with the Holy Spirit.

But a captain and lieutenant (ministers) whom I know found that "the vision tarried," so they waited for it and spent all the spare time they had for three weeks, crying to God to fill them with the Spirit. They did not get discouraged; they held on to God with a desperate faith. They would not let Him go, and they got their heart's desire. I saw that lieutenant some time afterward, and I was amazed at the wonders of God's grace in him. The spirit of the prophets was upon him.

"All heaven is free plunder to faith," says a friend of mine.

Oh, this waiting on God! It is far easier to plunge madly at this thing and that, and do, do, do, until life and heart are exhausted in joyless and comparatively fruitless toil, than it is to wait on God in patient faith until He comes and fills you with the power of the Holy Spirit. It is the Spirit that gives you supernatural endurance and wisdom and might, enables you to do in a day what otherwise you could not do in a thousand years (yet strips you of all pride), and leads you to give all the glory to your Lord.

Waiting on God empties us that we may be filled. Few wait until they are emptied, and hence few are filled. Few will bear the heart searchings, the humiliations, the suspense, the taunt of Satan as he inquires, "Where is your God now?" Oh, the questionings and whisperings of unbelief that are involved in waiting upon God, hence the few who, in understanding, are men and women in Christ Jesus and pillars in the temple of God.

Jesus commanded the disciples, and said: "Tarry in the city of Jerusalem until you are endued with power from on high" (Luke 24:49 NKJV). That must have been quite a restraint put on restless, impulsive Peter; but he waited with his brothers and sisters, and they cried to God, searched their hearts, and forgot their fears and the angry rulers who had murdered their Lord. They forgot their jealousies and selfish ambitions and childish differences, until they were exhausted of all self-love and self-goodness and self-trust, their hearts were as the heart of one man, and they had but one desire—a mighty, consuming hunger for God. Then suddenly God came—in power, with fire, to purge, cleanse, and sanctify them through and through, and to dwell in their hearts and make them bold in the presence of their enemies, humble in the midst of success, patient in fiery conflicts and persecutions, steadfast and unswerving in spite of threats and whippings and imprisonment, joyful in loneliness and misrepresentations, and fearless and triumphant in the face of death. God made them wise to win souls and filled them with the very spirit of their Master, till they turned the world upside down and took none of the glory to themselves, either.

So, sanctification is the result of not only giving, but also receiving. And we are under as solemn an obligation to receive the Holy Spirit and "be filled with the Spirit" (Eph. 5:18 KJV) as we are to give ourselves to God. If we are not filled at once, we are not to suppose that the blessing is not for us and, in the subtle, mock humility of unbelief, fold our hands and stop our crying to God. But we should cry all the more, and search the Scriptures, and search and humble ourselves, and take God's part against unbelief, and never faint until we have taken the kingdom of heaven by storm and He says to us, "Your faith is great. Your request is granted" (Matt. 15:28 NLT).

God *loves* to be compelled. God *wants* to be compelled. God *will* be compelled by the persistent prayer and faith of His children. I imagine God is often grieved and disappointed and angry with us, as the prophet was with the king who shot only three arrows when he should have shot half a dozen or more (see 2 Kings 13), because we ask so little, are so easily turned away without the blessing we profess to want, and are so quickly satisfied with a little comfort when it is the Comforter Himself we need.

The woman who came to Jesus to have the Devil cast out of her daughter is a sample believer and puts most Christians to shame by the boldness and persistence of her faith. She would not be turned away without the blessing she sought. At first, Jesus answered her not a word, and so He often treats us today. We pray and get no answer. God is silent. Then He rebuffed her by saying that He had not come to such as she, but to the lost sheep of the house of Israel. That was enough to make blaspheming skeptics of most modern folks. But not so with her. Her desperate faith grew awfully sublime. At last, Jesus seemed to add insult to injury by declaring, "It isn't right to take food from the children and throw it to the dogs" (Matt. 15:26 NLT).

Then the woman's faith conquered and compelled Him, for she said, "That's true, Lord, but even dogs are allowed to eat the scraps that fall beneath their masters' table" (Matt. 15:27 NLT). She was willing to take the dogs' place and receive the dogs' portion. Oh, how her faith triumphed, and Jesus, amazed, said, "O woman, great is your faith! Be it done for you as you desire" (Matt. 15:28 ESV). Jesus meant to bless her all the time, if her faith would hold out. And so He means to bless you.

There are two classes of people who progress to consecrate themselves to God, but upon inquiry it will usually appear that they are consecrated to something other than God Himself. They are God's housekeepers, rather than the bride of His Son—very busy people, with little or no time nor inclination for real heart fellowship with Jesus.

The first class might be termed pleasure seekers. They see that sanctified people are happy, and, thinking it is due to what they have given and done, they begin to give and to do, never dreaming of the infinite Treasure these sanctified ones have received. The secret of him who said, "The Lord is the portion of my soul," is hidden from them. So they never find God. They are seeking happiness, not holiness. They are usually good livers, hearty eaters, very sociable, always dressed in the latest fashion—religious epicures. They will hardly admit their need of holiness—they were always good—and God is found only by those who, feeling the deep depravity and need of their hearts, want to be holy. "Blessed are those who hunger and thirst for righteousness, for they will be filled" (Matt. 5:6 NIV).

The other class may be rightly called misery hunters. They are always seeking something hard to do. They believe in being on the rack perpetually. Like Baal's priests, they cut themselves—not their bodies, but their minds and souls. They give their goods to feed the poor, they give their bodies to be burned, and yet it profits them nothing (see 1 Cor. 13:3). They wear themselves out in a hard bond service. It is not joy they want, but misery. They judge their acceptance with God, not by the joy-producing presence of the indwelling Comforter that makes the yoke easy and the burden light, but rather by the amount of misery they are ready to endure or have endured. They are not happy, and they fear they are not saved, unless there is some sacrifice for them to make that will produce in them the most exquisite torment. They have died a thousand deaths, and yet are not dead. Their religion does not consist in "righteousness and peace and joy in the Holy Spirit" (Rom. 14:17 ESV) but rather in grit and resolution and misery.

These people do not really make greater sacrifices than sanctified people; they merely make more ado over them. Not being dead, it hurts them to submit to God, and yet they feel compelled to do so. Nor are their sorrows greater than those of sanctified people; they are merely of a different kind and spring from a different root. They have misery and sorrow because of the sacrifices they have to make, while the sanctified soul counts these things all joy for Jesus' sake (while feeling continual sorrow for woes of the world which, but for the comfort and sympathy Jesus gives, would break his or her heart).

Still, these people are good and do good, God bless them! But what they need is a faith that sanctifies (see Acts 26:18), a faith that through the operation of the Spirit will kill them, put them out of their misery forever, and bring joy and peace into their tired hearts, so that in newness of life they can drink from the river of God's pleasures, never thirst anymore, and make all manner of sacrifices for Jesus' sake with utter gladness.

It is sanctification, then, that we need, that God wants us to have, and that the Holy Spirit is urging upon every one of us. It is a way of childlike faith that receives all God has to give, and of perfect love that joyfully gives all back to God. It is a way that keeps the soul from sloth and ease on the one hand, and from hard, cold bondage on the other. It is a way of inward peace and pleasantness and abounding spiritual life, in which the soul, always wary of its enemies, is not unduly elated by success nor cast down by disappointment. It is a way that does not measure itself by others, nor compare itself with others, but, looking to Jesus, attends strictly to its own business, walking by faith, and trusting Him in due time and order to fulfill all the exceeding great and precious promises of His love.

Shouting  27

Nothing is more completely hidden from wise and prudent folk than the blessed fact that there is a secret spring of power and victory in shouting and praising God.

The Devil often throws a spell over people that can be broken in no other way. Many honest, seeking souls, who might step forth into perfect and perpetual liberty if they would only dare to look the Devil in the eye and shout, "Glory to God!" go mourning all their days under this spell. Frequently whole congregations will be under it. There will be a vacant or a listless or a restless look in their eyes. There is no attention, no expectation. A stifling stillness and "the serenity of death" settles upon them. But let a Spirit-baptized person with a weight of glory in the soul bless the Lord, and the spell will be broken. Everyone there will come to their senses, wake up, remember where they are, and begin to expect something to happen.

Shouting and praising God is to salvation what flame is to fire. You may have a very hot and useful fire without a blaze, but not until it bursts forth into flame does it become irresistible and sweep everything before it. So people may be very good and have an experience of salvation, but it is not until they become so full of the Holy Spirit that they are likely to burst forth in praises to their glorious God at any hour of the day or night, both in private and public, that their salvation becomes irresistibly contagious.

The shouting of some people is as terrible as the noise of an empty wagon rolling over cobblestones. It is like the firing of blank cartridges. It is all noise. Their religion consists in making a racket. But there are others who wait on God in secret places, who seek His face with their whole hearts, who groan in prayer with unutterable longing to know God in all His fullness and to see His kingdom come with power, who plead the promises, who search the Word of God and meditate on it day and night until they are full of the great thoughts and truths of God and faith is made perfect. Then the Holy Spirit comes pressing down on them with an eternal weight of glory that compels praise, and when they shout it takes effect. Every cartridge is loaded, and at times their shouting will be like the boom of a big gun and will have the speed and power of a cannonball.

An old friend of mine in Vermont once remarked that when he went into a store or railway station, he found the place full of devils, and the atmosphere choked his soul till he shouted. Then every devil sped away, the atmosphere was purified, and he had possession of the place and could say and do what he pleased.

Catherine Booth-Clibborn, who pioneered The Salvation Army in France, once wrote, "Nothing fills all hell with dismay like a reckless, daredevil shouting faith." Nothing can stand before someone with a genuine shout in his or her soul. Earth and hell flee before such a person, and all heaven throngs around to help fight that person's battles.

When Joshua's armies shouted, the walls of Jericho fell down flat before them. When Jehoshaphat's people "began to sing and to praise, the LORD set ambushes against the people of Ammon, Moab, and Mount Seir" (2 Chron. 20:22 NKJV), and God's enemies were routed. When Paul and Silas, with bruised and bleeding backs, in the inner dungeon of that horrible Philippian jail at midnight, "prayed, and sang praises unto God" (Acts 16:25 KJV), the Lord sent an earthquake, shook the foundations of the prison, loosed the prisoners, and redeemed the jailer and all his family. And there is no conceivable difficulty that will not vanish before the person who prays and praises God.

When the Cornish evangelist Billy Bray wanted bread, he prayed and shouted to get the Devil to understand that he felt under no obligation to him but had perfect confidence in his heavenly Father. When Dr. Charles Cullis had not a penny in his treasury and heavy obligations for his home for consumptives rested upon him, and he knew not how he could buy food for the patients, he would go into his office and read the Bible and pray and walk the floor, praising God and telling Him he would trust. And money would roll in from the ends of the earth. Victory always comes where someone, having poured out his or her heart in prayer, dares to trust God and express his or her faith in praise.

Shouting is the final and highest expression of faith made perfect in its various stages. When a soul comes to God in hearty repentance and surrender, and, throwing him- or herself fully on the mercy of God, looks to Jesus only for salvation, and by faith fully and fearlessly grasps the blessing of justification, the first expression of that faith will be one of confidence and praise. No doubt there are many who claim justification who never praise God. But either they are deceived or their faith is weak and mixed with doubt and fear. When it is perfect, praise will be spontaneous.

And when regenerate souls come to see the holiness of God, the exceeding breadth of His commandment, and His absolute claim upon every power of their being, and realize the remaining selfishness and earthiness of their hearts—and when they, after many failures to purify themselves and inward questionings of soul and debatings of conscience and haltings of faith, come to God to be made holy through the precious blood and the baptism of the Holy Spirit and of fire—the final expression of the faith that resolutely and perfectly grasps the blessing will not be prayer, but praise and hallelujahs.

And when such saved and sanctified men and women, seeing the woes of a lost world and feeling the holy passion of Jesus working mightily in them, go forth to war "against evil rulers and authorities of the unseen world, against mighty powers in this dark world, and against evil spirits in the heavenly places" (Eph. 6:12 NLT), in order to rescue the slaves of sin and hell, after weeping and agonizing in prayer to God for an outpouring of the Spirit, preaching to and teaching others, pleading with them to yield utterly to God, and after many fastings and trials and conflicts in which faith and patience for others are made perfect and victorious, prayer will be transformed into praise, weeping into shouting, and apparent defeat into overwhelming victory!

Where there is victory, there is shouting. And where there is no shouting, faith and patience are either in retreat or are engaged in conflict,
the conclusion of which for the time being seems uncertain.

> Oh, for a faith that will not shrink
> Though pressed by every foe,
> That will not tremble on the brink
> Of any earthly woe.
> Faith, mighty faith, the promise sees,
> And looks to that alone,
> Laughs at impossibilities,
> And cries, "It shall be done!"[1]

And what is true in individual experience is revealed to be true of
the church in its final triumph. For after the long ages of stress and
conflict and patient waiting and fiery trial, after the ceaseless intercessions of Jesus and the unutterable groaning of the Spirit in the hearts
of believers, the church shall finally come to perfect faith and patience
and unity of love, according to the prayer of Jesus in John 17. Then
"the Lord himself will come down from heaven with a commanding
shout, with the voice of the archangel, and with the trumpet call of God"
(1 Thess. 4:16 NLT), and seeming defeat shall be turned into eternal
victory.

But let no one hastily conclude that we should not shout and praise
God unless we feel a mighty wave of triumph rushing through our
soul. Paul said, "We don't know what God wants us to pray for. But
the Holy Spirit prays for us with groanings that cannot be expressed

in words" (Rom. 8:26 NLT). But if we refused to pray till we felt this tremendous pleading of the Spirit in our hearts (which John Fletcher said is "like a God wrestling with a God"[2]), we would never pray at all. We must stir up the gift of prayer that is within us, we must exercise ourselves in prayer until our souls sweat, and then we shall realize the mighty energy of the Holy Spirit interceding within us. We must never forget that "the spirits of prophets are subject to the prophets" (1 Cor. 14:32 NRSV). Just so we must stir up and exercise the gift of praise within us.

We must put our will into it. When Habakkuk the prophet had lost everything and was surrounded with utter desolation, he shouted, "Yet I will rejoice in the LORD, I will joy in the God of my salvation!" (Hab. 3:18 KJV). We are workers together with God, and if we will praise Him, He will see to it that we have something for which to praise Him. We often hear of Daniel praying three times a day, but we pass over the fact that at the same time he "gave thanks before his God" (Dan. 6:10 KJV), which is a kind of praise. David said, "I will praise you seven times a day" (Ps. 119:164 NLT). Over and over, again and again, we are exhorted and commanded to praise God and shout aloud and rejoice evermore. But if through fear or shame we will not rejoice, we need not be surprised that we have no joy and no sweeping victories.

But if we will get alone with God in our own hearts (note: alone with God in our own hearts; there is the place to get alone with God, and a shout is nothing more or less than an expression of joy at finding God in our hearts) and will praise Him for His wonderful works, praise Him because He is worthy of praise, praise Him whether we feel like it or not, praise Him in the darkness as well as the light, praise Him in seasons of fierce conflict as well as in moments of victory, we will soon be able to shout aloud for joy. And our joy no one will be able to take from us, but God will cause us to drink of the river of His pleasures, and He himself will be our "exceeding joy" (Ps. 43:4 KJV).

Many a soul in fierce temptation and hellish darkness has poured out his or her heart in prayer and then sunk back in despair, who, if he or she had only closed the prayer with thanks and dared in the name of God to shout, would have filled hell with confusion and won a victory that would have struck all the harps of heaven and made the angels shout with glee. Many a prayer meeting has failed at the shouting point. Songs were sung, testimonies given, the Bible read and explained, wayward souls warned and entreated, and prayers poured forth to God, but no one wrestled through to the point where he or she could and would intelligently praise God for victory, and, so far as could be seen, the battle was lost for want of a shout.

From the moment we are born of God, straight through our pilgrim journey, up to the moment of open vision where we are forever glorified and see Jesus as He is, we have a right to rejoice, and we ought to do it. It is our highest privilege and our most solemn duty. And if we do it not, I think it must fill the angels with confusion and the fiends of the bottomless pit with a kind of hideous joy. We ought to do it, for this is almost the only thing we do on earth that we shall not cease to do in heaven. Weeping, fasting, watching, praying, self-denying, cross-bearing, and being in conflict with hell will cease; but praise to God and hallelujahs "to him who loves us and has freed us from our sins by his blood, and has made us to be a kingdom and priests to serve his God and Father" (Rev. 1:5–6 NIV) shall ring through heaven eternally.

NOTES

1. Charles Wesley, "Father of Jesus Christ, My Lord," 1742, public domain.

2. John Fletcher, *The Works of the Rev. John Fletcher, Late Vicar of Madeley*, vol. 1 (London: John Mason, 1859), 195.

Some of God's Words to Me

God did not cease speaking to humankind when the canon of Scripture was complete. Though the manner of communication may have changed somewhat, the communication itself is something to which every Spirit-born soul can joyfully testify. Everyone who is sorry for sin, sighing and crying for deliverance, and hungering and thirsting for righteousness, will soon find out, as did the Israelites, that "God can speak to us humans" (Deut. 5:24 NLT).

God has most commonly and most powerfully spoken to me through the words of Scripture. Some of them stand out to my mental and spiritual vision like mighty mountain peaks, rising from a vast, extended plain. The Spirit that moved "holy men of God" (2 Pet. 1:21 KJV) to write the words of the Bible has moved me to understand them by leading me along the lines of spiritual experience first trodden by these men, and has taken the things of Christ and revealed them to me, until I have been filled with a divine certainty as altogether satisfactory and absolute as the certainty produced in my intellect by a mathematical demonstration.

The first words I remember coming to me with this irresistible divine force came when I was seeking the blessing of a clean heart. Although I was hungering and thirsting for the blessing, yet at times a feeling of utter indifference—a kind of spiritual stupor—would come over me and threaten to devour all my holy longings, as the lean cows in Pharaoh's dream devoured the fat ones (see Gen. 41). I was in great distress and did not know what to do. I saw that to stop seeking meant infinite, eternal loss. Yet to continue seeking seemed quite out of the question with such a paralysis of desire and feeling. But one day I read, "There is no one who calls on Your name, who stirs himself up to take hold of You" (Isa. 64:7 NKJV).

God spoke to me in these words as unmistakably as He spoke to Moses from the burning bush or the children of Israel from the cloudy mount. It was an altogether new experience to me. The word came as a rebuke to my unbelief and lazy indifference, and yet it put hope into me, and I said to myself, "By the grace of God, if nobody else does I will stir myself up to seek Him, feeling or no feelings."

That was ten years ago, but from then till now, regardless of my feeling, I have sought God. I have not waited to be stirred up, but when necessary I have fasted and prayed and stirred myself up. I have often prayed, as did the royal psalmist, "Make me live again, LORD, according to your faithful love" (Ps. 119:159 CEB). But whether I have felt any immediate results or not, I have laid hold of Him, sought Him, and found Him. "Seek, and you will find" (Matt. 7:7 ESV).

Because hindrances must be removed before we can ever find God in the fullness of His love and favor, weights and easily-besetting sins must be laid aside (see Heb. 12:1), and self must be smitten in the citadel of its ambitions and hopes.

Young men and women today are ambitious. They want to be prime minister if they go into politics. They must be multimillionaires if they go into business. They aim to become a bishop if they pursue ministry in the church.

The ruling passion of my soul (and that which for years I longed after more than for holiness or heaven) was to do something and be somebody who should win the esteem and compel the applause of thoughtful, educated people. And just as the angel smote Jacob's thigh and put it out of joint, causing him forever after to limp on it, the strongest part of his body, so God, in order to sanctify me wholly and bring "into captivity every thought to the obedience of Christ" (2 Cor. 10:5 KJV), smote and humbled me in this ruling propensity and strongest passion of my nature.

For several years before God sanctified me wholly, I knew there was such an experience, and I prayed by fits and starts for it, and all the time I hungered and thirsted for—I hardly knew what! Holiness in itself seemed desirable, but I saw as clearly then as I have since I obtained the blessing that with it came the cross and an irrepressible conflict with the carnal mind in each human being I met, whether that person was a professed Christian or an avowed sinner, whether cultured and thoughtful or a raw and ignorant pagan. And this I knew instinctively would as surely bar my way to the esteem and applause of the people whose goodwill and admiration I valued, as it did that of Jesus and Paul. And yet, so subtle is the deceitfulness of the unsanctified heart, that I would not then have acknowledged it to myself, although I am now persuaded that unwillingness to take up this cross was for years the lurking foe that barred the gates against the willing, waiting Sanctifier.

~ However, at last I heard a distinguished evangelist and soul-winner preach a sermon on the baptism of the Holy Spirit, and I said to myself, "That is what I need and want; I must have it!" And I began to seek and pray for this, all the time with a secret thought in my heart that I, too, should become a great soul-winner and live in the eye of the world. I sought with considerable earnestness, but God was very merciful and hid Himself from me, thus arousing the wholesome fear of the Lord in my heart and at the same time intensifying my spiritual hunger. I wept and prayed and begged the Lord to baptize me with the Spirit, and wondered why He did not, until one day I read those words of Paul: "That no flesh should glory in his presence" (1 Cor. 1:29 KJV).

Here I saw the enemy of the Lord: self. There stood the idol of my soul—the passionate, consuming desire for glory—no longer hidden and nourished in the secret chambers of my heart, but discovered before the Lord as the Amalekite king Agag was before Samuel (see 1 Sam. 15). And those words, "No flesh should glory in his presence," constituted "the sword of the Spirit" (Eph. 6:17 KJV) which pierced self through and through, and showed me I never could be holy and receive the baptism of the Spirit while I secretly cherished a desire for the honor that comes from others and sought not "the honor that comes from the one who alone is God" (John 5:44 NLT). That word came to me with power, and from then till now I have not sought the glory of this world. But while I no longer sought the glory of the world, yet this same powerful principle in me still had to be further uncovered and smitten, in order to make me willing to lose what little glory I already had (or imagined I had) and be content to be accounted a fool for Christ.

The ruling propensity of the carnal nature seeks gratification. If it can secure this lawfully, it will. But gratification it will have, even if it has to gain it unlawfully. Every way is unlawful for me which would be unlawful for Jesus. Christians who are not entirely sanctified do not deliberately plan to do what they know to be wrong, but are rather betrayed by the deceitful heart within. If they are overcome (which, thank God, they need not be), they are overcome secretly or suddenly, in a way that makes them abhor themselves, but which, it seems, is the only way by which God can convince them of their depravity and need of a clean heart.

I was so betrayed on two occasions—once to cheat on an examination, and once to use the outline of another man's sermon. The first deed I bitterly repented of and confessed but the second was not so clearly wrong, since I had used materials of my own to fill in an outline, and especially since the outline was probably much better than any I could prepare (it was one of Charles Finney's outlines). In fact, if I had used the outline in the right spirit, I do not know that it would have been wrong at all. But God's Word, which is a "discerner of the thoughts and intents of the heart" (Heb. 4:12 KJV), searched me out and revealed to my astonished, humbled soul not merely the bearing and character of my act, but also of my spirit. He smote and humbled me again with these words: "If anyone speaks, they should do so as one who speaks the very words of God. If anyone serves, they should do so with the strength God provides" (1 Pet. 4:11 NIV).

When I read those words, I felt as low and guilty as though I had stolen ten thousand dollars. I began to see then the true character and mission of preachers and prophets, who are men and women sent from God and who must, if they would please God and seek the glory He alone gives, wait upon God in prayer and diligent searching of His Word till they get the message direct from the throne. Then only can they speak "as one who speaks the very words of God" and serve "with the strength God provides." I was not led to despise human teachers and human learning where God is in them, but I was led to exalt direct inspiration and to see the absolute necessity of it for everyone who sets him- or herself to turn people's hearts to righteousness and tell them how to find God and get to heaven. I saw that instead of always sitting at the feet of human teachers, poring over commentaries, studying someone else's sermons, diving into others' volumes of anecdotes, and then tickling the ears of people with pretty speeches and winning their fleeting, empty applause by elaborately finished sermons, logically and rhetorically "faultily faultless, icily regular, splendidly null,"[1] God meant me to speak His words, to sit at the feet of Jesus and learn of Him, to get alone in some secret place on my knees and study the Word of God under the direct illumination of the Holy Spirit, to study the holiness and righteous judgments of God until I got some red hot thunderbolts that would burn the itching ears of the people, arouse their slumbering consciences, prick their hard hearts, and make them cry, "What shall we do?" (Acts 2:37 KJV).

I saw that I must study and meditate on the tender, boundless compassion and love of God in Christ, the perfect atonement for sin in its root and trunk and branch, and the simple way to appropriate it in penitence and self-surrender by faith, until I was fully possessed of it myself and knew how to lead every broken heart directly to Jesus for perfect healing, to comfort mourners, to loose prisoners, to set captives free, and to proclaim the acceptable year of the Lord and the day of vengeance of our God.

This view greatly humbled me, and I did not know what to do. At last it was suggested to my mind that, as I had confessed the false examination, so now I ought to stand before the people and confess the stolen sermon outline. This fairly peeled my conscience, and it quivered with an indescribable agony. For about three weeks I struggled with this problem. I argued the matter with myself. I pleaded with God to show me if it was His will, and over and over again I promised Him I would do it, only to draw back in my heart. At last I told an intimate friend. He assured me it was not of God and said he was going to preach in a revival meeting that night and use materials he had gathered from another man's sermon. I coveted his freedom, but this brought no relief to me. I could not get away from my sin. Like David's, it was "ever before me" (Ps. 51:3 KJV).

One morning, while in this frame of mind, I picked up a little book on experimental religion, hoping to get light. On opening it, the very first subject my eyes fell on was confession. I was cornered. My soul was brought to a full halt. I could seek no further light. I wanted to die, and that moment my heart broke within me: "The sacrifices of God are a broken spirit: a broken and a contrite heart" (Ps. 51:17 KJV).

From the depths of my broken heart, my conquered spirit said to God, "I will." I had said it before with my lips, but now I said it with my heart. Then God spoke directly to my soul, not by printed words through my eyes but by His Spirit in my heart: "If we confess our sins, he is faithful and just to forgive us our sins, and to cleanse us from all unrighteousness" (1 John 1:9 KJV). The first part about forgiveness I knew, but the last clause about cleansing was a revelation to me. I did not remember ever having seen or heard it before. The word came with power, and I bowed my head in my hands and said, "Father, I believe that." Then a great rest came into my soul, and I knew I was clean. In that instant, "the blood of Christ, who through the eternal Spirit offered himself without spot to God, [purged my] conscience from dead works to serve the living God" (Heb. 9:14 KJV).

God did not require Abraham to slay Isaac. All He wanted was a willing heart. So He did not require me to confess to the people. When my heart was willing, He swept the whole subject out of my mind and freed me utterly from slavish fear. My idol—self—was gone. God knew I withheld nothing from Him, so He filled my soul with peace and showed me that "Christ is the end of the law for righteousness to everyone who believes" (Rom. 10:4 NASB) and that the whole will of God was summed up in five words: "Faith expressing itself in love" (Gal. 5:6 NLT).

Shortly after this, I ran into my friend's room with a borrowed book. The moment his eyes fell upon me, he said, "What is the matter? Something has happened to you." My face was witnessing to a pure heart before my lips did. But my lips soon followed and have continued to this day.

The psalmist said, "I have told the glad news of deliverance in the great congregation; behold, I have not restrained my lips, as you know, O LORD. I have not hidden your deliverance within my heart; I have spoken of your faithfulness and your salvation; I have not concealed your steadfast love and your faithfulness from the great congregation" (Ps. 40:9–10 ESV).

Satan hates holy testimony, and he nearly entrapped me after I received the blessing of holiness. I felt I ought to preach it, but I shrank from the podium and the conflict I saw it would surely bring, and I hesitated to declare publicly that I was sanctified, for fear of doing more harm than good. I saw only reproach. The glory that was to follow was hidden from my eyes. Beautiful, flowery sermons that appealed to the imagination and aroused the emotions, with just enough thought to properly balance them, were my ideal. I shrank from coming down to plain, heart-searching talks that laid hold of the consciences of men and women and made saints of them, or turned them into foes as implacable as the Pharisees were to Jesus or the Jews to Paul. But before I got the blessing, God held me to it, and I had promised God I would preach it if He would give me the experience. It was Friday that He cleansed me, and I determined to preach about it on the following Sunday. But I felt weak and faint.

On Saturday morning, however, I met a noisy, shouting coachman on the street, who had the blessing, and I told him what God had done for me. He shouted and praised God, and said, "Now, Brother Brengle, you preach it. The church is dying for this."

We walked across Boston Common and Garden and talked about the matter, and my heart burned within me as did the hearts of the two disciples with whom Jesus talked on the road to Emmaus. In my inmost soul I recounted the cost, threw in my lot with Jesus crucified, and determined I would teach holiness even if it banished me forever from the pulpit and made me a byword to all my acquaintances. Then I felt strong. The way to get strength is to throw yourself away for Jesus.

The next day I went to my church and preached as best I could out of a two-days-old experience, from "Let us go on unto perfection" (Heb. 6:1 KJV). I closed with my experience, and the people broke down and wept, and some came to me afterward and said they wanted that same experience, and some of them got it! I did not know what I was doing that morning, but I knew afterward. I was burning up my ships and casting down my bridges behind me. I was now in the Enemy's land, fully committed to a warfare of utter extermination to all sin. I was on record now before heaven, earth, and hell. Angels, mortals, and devils had heard my testimony, and I must go forward or openly and ignominiously retreat in the face of a jeering foe. I see now that there is a divine philosophy in requiring us not only to believe with our hearts unto righteousness, but to confess with the mouth unto salvation (see Rom. 10:10). God led me along these lines. No one taught me.

After I had put myself on record, I walked softly with God, desiring nothing but His will and looking to Him to keep me every instant. I did not know there was anything more for me, but I meant, by God's grace, to hold what I had by doing His will as He had made it known to me and by trusting Him with all my heart.

But God meant greater things for me. On the following Tuesday morning, just after rising, with a heart full of eager desire for God, I read these words of Jesus at the grave of Lazarus: "I am the resurrection and the life. Anyone who believes in me will live, even after dying. Everyone who lives in me and believes in me will never ever die. Do you believe this?" (John 11:25–26 NLT). The Holy Spirit, the other "Comforter," was in those words, and in an instant my soul melted before the Lord like wax before fire, and I knew Jesus. He was revealed in me as He had promised, and I loved Him with an unutterable love. I wept and adored and loved and loved and loved. I walked out over Boston Common before breakfast, and still wept and adored and loved. Talk about the occupation of heaven! I do not know what it will be—though, of course, it will be suited to, and commensurate with, our redeemed capacities and powers—but I knew this then, that if I could lie prostrate at the feet of Jesus for all eternity and love and adore Him, I would be satisfied. My soul was satisfied, satisfied, satisfied!

That experience fixed my theology. From then till now, mortals and devils might as well try to get me to question the presence of the sun in the heavens as to question the existence of God, the divinity of Jesus Christ, and the sanctifying power of an ever present, almighty Holy Spirit. I am as sure the Bible is the Word of God as I am of my own existence, while heaven and hell are as much realities to me as day and night, winter and summer, or good and evil. I feel the powers of the world to come and the pull of heaven in my own soul.

It is some years now since the Comforter came, and He abides in me still. He has not stopped speaking to me yet. He has set my soul on fire, but, like the burning bush Moses saw in the Mount, it is not consumed.

To all who want such an experience I would say, "Ask, and it shall be given you" (Matt. 7:7 KJV). If it does not come for the asking, "keep on seeking, and you will find" (Matt. 7:7 NLT). If it is still delayed, "keep on knocking, and the door will be opened to you" (Matt. 7:7 NLT). In other words, seek until you have sought with your whole heart, and there and then you will find Him. "Stop doubting and believe" (John 20:27 NIV). "If you will not believe, surely you shall not be established" (Isa. 7:9 NKJV).

I do not consider myself beyond the possibility of falling. I know I stand by faith and must watch and pray lest I enter into temptation, and take heed lest I fall. Yet, in view of all God's marvelous loving kindnesses and tender mercies to me, I constantly sing, with the apostle Jude: "Now unto him that is able to keep you from falling, and to present you faultless before the presence of his glory with exceeding joy, to the only wise God our Saviour, be glory and majesty, dominion and power, both now and ever. Amen" (Jude 24–25 KJV).

NOTE

1. Alfred Lord Tennyson, "Maud," *English Poetry III: From Tennyson to Whitman*, The Harvard Classics, vol. 42 (New York: P. F. Collier & Son, 1909–1914), n.p.

Samuel L. Brengle's Holy Life Series

This series comprises the complete works of Samuel L. Brengle, combining all nine of his original books into six volumes, penned by one of the great minds on holiness. Each volume has been lovingly edited for modern readership by popular author (and long-time Brengle devotee) Bob Hostetler. Brengle's authentic voice remains strong, now able to more relevantly engage today's disciples of holiness. These books are must-haves for all who would seriously pursue and understand the depths of holiness in the tradition of John Wesley.

Helps to Holiness
ISBN: 978-1-63257-064-2
eBook: 978-1-63257-065-9

The Heart of Holiness
ISBN: 978-1-63257-066-6
eBook: 978-1-63257-067-3

The Servant's Heart
ISBN: 978-1-63257-068-0
eBook: 978-1-63257-069-7

Ancient Prophets and Modern Problems
ISBN: 978-1-63257-070-3
eBook: 978-1-63257-071-0

Come Holy Guest
ISBN: 978-1-63257-072-7
eBook: 978-1-63257-073-4

Resurrection Life and Power
ISBN: 978-1-63257-074-1
eBook: 978-1-63257-075-8

**Samuel L. Brengle's
Holy Life Series Box Set**
ISBN: 978-1-63257-076-5